WHEN A CHILD DIES

When a Child Dies

Footsteps of a Grieving Family

JIM O'SHEA

VERITAS

Published 2008 by
Veritas Publications
7/8 Lower Abbey Street
Dublin 1
Ireland

Email publications@veritas.ie
Website www.veritas.ie

ISBN 978-1-184730-078-2

A catalogue record for this book is available from the British Library.

Designed by Lir Mac Cárthaigh
Printed in Ireland by Betaprint, Dublin

Veritas books are printed on paper made from the wood pulp of managed forests. For every tree felled, at least one tree is planted, thereby renewing natural resources.

Contents

Introduction

In talking about the death of a child, I wish to be as inclusive as possible. Pre-natal and post-natal children, miscarried children, children who die in the womb, still-births, children who die soon after birth, pre-teen and teenagers, and adult children of all ages are relevant to the context of this book. To lose a child is one of the most devastating ordeals a family can suffer. Our children have said that they cannot imagine how painful it is for Mary and me, as parents, to have lost our child. Breda, one of our daughters, cannot find words to express how sad she is for us that we were to 'fall in love, carry a baby for nine months, give birth, and then lose that person you created together. To have him snatched away years before his time'. That may be so, and there is no point in trying to compare the severity of grief, but having read the anguish that my surviving children suffered, I can only conclude that the pain of siblings is far more severe than what we may imagine.

The sudden death of a child creates chaos in a family, and the family must struggle through this chaos before beginning their grieving process. We experienced this chaos on Sunday 18 February 1990 when our youngest child, Cathal, was killed on the road outside our house. He was only thirteen, still innocent, full of fun, a kind and caring child. For some time I have considered writing an account of how we dealt with the chaotic situation we found ourselves in, and how we coped with the overwhelming sense of loss, especially in the early days. It is only now, after a long period of training to be a counsellor, that I can contemplate such an undertaking. As part of my counselling training I did considerable research on grief and bereavement for my thesis. Some of the material I read was entirely academic, explaining the feelings of grief, and the tasks of grieving; others had a more human touch and were a celebration of the deceased. When I wrote my thesis I combined the two, but it still had a largely academic bias, and would have been of limited help to those suffering loss.

This account is neither of these two approaches. It is not about Cathal. It is about our experience of losing him. It is about the brutality of sudden death. It is not embellished in any way, and it is not an exercise in self-pity. It shows what happened and how we experienced it. Writing the book has been a more painful experience than I anticipated, and I hope it will help my family as well as others who read it. Although I am the author, every member of the family has contibuted. Their written accounts show how differently people grieve. Some of my family have come to terms with this most painful loss better than others. As far as I can see, this is one of the few books that allows male and female siblings to express in their own words how the death of a sibling affected them. Any books I have read on the death of a child use parents' accounts of how their surviving children subsequently felt. This book will show the feelings of siblings in their teens and early twenties, and later on as mature adults. Bill was only seventeen when Cathal died, Deirdre was nineteen, Breda was twenty-one, and Frances twenty-two.

People say that one never gets over the death of a child. I never wanted to believe this. It is possible to get over many losses, and I thought that the loss of a child was no exception. This thought, in a sense, was a burden. This burden was lifted one day when a psychotherapist friend remarked that one never really gets over the death of a child. She did not realise how her comment impacted on me. But I believed her because she is a highly skilled therapist with long experience, and it validated how I felt, so long after Cathal had died. It made me accept the reality that I had been trying to dismiss, pretending that after a number of years I could be perfectly happy, even though I knew deep down that I would never forget. Of course, there is no forgetting, and there is sometimes some element of pain, as I suspect there will be for as long as I live. There will always be a nagging feeling of loss, some unease beneath the surface. It is not always apparent, but it is never absent. There is no perfect happiness following the death of a child.

So now when people ask me if it is possible to get over the death of a child, my response is that it is not, but that the surviving parents and siblings can be peaceful and happy. That is how I am. I am happy, and have peace of mind. But I think of Cathal almost every day, even after eighteen years, and sometimes I feel a deep sadness and a sense of loss. I think of Cathal because I always remember my family, alive and dead, in my brief daily prayers, and because the graveyard where he lies is on the road from my house to Thurles. I rarely visit his grave. The memory of him, his face and his voice, are engraved on my heart. Mary, however, finds some comfort in visiting his grave every Sunday. I know, too, that he is forever in her heart; she who remained at home from work so that she would always be there for him and for all our children.

Sometimes I remember him as I pass the crossroads where he was killed. At one stage I contemplated putting up a cross where he died. I wanted people to remember what had happened. I wanted people to know that we had lost a child.

I actually received permission from the County Manager to do so. This thinking soon changed. As I have said, Cathal is always in my heart; I don't need any concrete reminders of him. He lives there, always as a thirteen-year-old child. He will never grow old for us. I do not always feel sad when I see reminders of Cathal, but probably a little numb, for it is still hard to contemplate the loss of my child. It is hard to contemplate this young boy lying in the cold earth, as I drive past the graveyard. It is not possible to forget. But who would want to forget one's child? These moments of sadness are generally brief, and I rarely think of him for the rest of the day. Life goes on, and most of the time is happy and peaceful.

My main purpose in writing the book is to give bereaved parents and siblings hope. As a former school principal, I have encountered many bereaved teenagers. I have experienced a child die in the school, and another die on the day before the school opened for the new scholastic year. When I was doing my thesis a group of children in Transition Year produced a number of creative pieces showing how they had grieved. I was amazed and moved by these creations. I really would have liked to let them know that I understood what was happening for them. Understanding by others is so important in the healing process. I hope this book will show others that my children suffered as much as Mary and I did, and that this will validate the feelings, thoughts and behaviours of other bereaved children.

I hope, too, that it will validate the grief feelings, thoughts and behaviours of parents. Parents will always carry the memory of their child in their hearts. That child will be present at all major family occasions and anniversaries. Tears will be shed, thoughts perhaps unspoken. But, peace and happiness will also be present, if, of course, the painful course of grief has been trodden, if the feelings of grief – shock, anger, loneliness, depression, sadness, guilt, self-reproach, helplessness, yearning – have been honoured, and perhaps challenged in the case of guilt or self-reproach. If these feelings are allowed, then the final stage of acceptance of some kind will come. That is the basic lesson of this book. But, how difficult it is to live in this pain! It is no wonder that many parents and siblings try to avoid it. Avoiding the pain of loss, however, simply prolongs the grieving, and is either like a psychological time bomb waiting to explode or a heavy cloud driving us into depression.

I considered shaping the book around themes, but I felt that this would make it academic. I have instead allowed my family members to speak for themselves. I have, however, looked at themes in the last chapter, drawing together our individual experiences and normalising them. Such normalisation of grief is important and helps healing. I decided to tell our story in as much detail as possible, using the three diaries kept by Mary, Breda, and myself, as well as written recollections from my family.

The book is about how our family members were devastated, experienced our grief, picked ourselves up and began to cope in our own individual ways. It is about individual as well as family grief. I hope that others will see parallels in their own grief trajectory. I hope, also, that it will help people who are suffering serious bereavement of any type, be it the loss of a child, parent, sibling, or someone close to them. Loss is painful, the feelings are the same for the survivors, but the loss of a child has a special dimension. In reading this book, my hope for bereaved people is that their tears are for their own loss and not for ours. We have trodden that painful path and people wept with us long ago when we needed such tears.

If any proof is needed that one heals, then this book is that proof. I, who at one time wondered how I would survive even an hour, can now write in detail about what happened eighteen years ago. This little work is proof that time does indeed heal. This healing preserves memories and integrates all the feelings of grief once experienced as trauma, but now as sadness.

There are certain aspects not covered here. It does not examine the pain and anguish inflicted on Cathal's aunts and uncles (Mary's brothers and sisters), who were so supportive to us in the years following his death. Neither does it look at the devastation caused to Cathal's friends, who not only saw him snatched by death, but saw their own mortality so cruelly exposed. It does not deal with the impact on his grandparents. All of these felt the great pain of loss. Their own suffering has in a sense gone unrecognised. I wish to recognise and acknowledge it here in this brief reference; and I would hope that someone may in the future write about how the wider family copes with the loss of a beloved relative. Their feelings also need to be validated.

I dedicate this book to my wife, Mary, to my children, to the wider family, to Cathal, and to his friends, who have seen how fragile life can be.

CHAPTER ONE

A Cloudless Horizon

A Family whose Youngest Child was Greatly Beloved

THE YEAR 1971 was a new and exciting one for our family. I resigned from Irish Shell and BP, where I had worked for five years. I had enjoyed working there, and I loved the Dublin of the 1960s, but I had always wished to live in the country, and it had long been my ambition to teach. I took up a teaching position in the Christian Brothers School in Thurles, my alma mater. I looked forward to living and working in my own county, Tipperary, and I felt that country life would give my children more freedom, remembering my own childhood in the beauty and wilderness of Kilcooley in the parish of Gurtnahoe, twelve miles from Thurles.

It was also, to my mind, a much safer place for children, with less road traffic. The place I chose to build my house, where Mary and I still live, is situated less than two miles from the town of Thurles, a rural setting on a back road. Indeed, a few miles further and the road has a ridge of grass growing right down the middle. There was little traffic on it in the 1970s. It was as safe a place for children as one could imagine.

We had three girls at that stage, Frances, Breda and Deirdre, all Dublin Jackeens, but who today profess to being loyal Tipperary women. Frances, the eldest, was only four years old, and had not yet started school. Two boys, Bill and

Cathal, were born to us in Thurles. Bill was born in 1972 and Cathal in 1976. Cathal arrived prematurely on Sunday 26 November 1976. We had been shopping in Thurles the day before when Mary suddenly felt some pain. As a precaution, we decided to go to the District Hospital, where they told us that she was in the early stages of labour and so couldn't leave. I dashed home in a panic and filled a suitcase with any clothes that looked as if they might be useful in hospital!

Our new baby spent the next six weeks or so in an incubator and we decided on the name 'Cathal'. It means 'strong in battle', and comes from the Gaelic word *cath*, meaning a battle. We thought about him all through Christmas, and looked forward to bringing him home in January. He looked so tiny in the incubator, and we longed to hold him. The nurses presented us with a caul, which had covered his head when he was born. We were so pleased at this. A caul is a membrane of skin, and is valued as a symbol of good luck. The Gaelic for caul is *caipín sonais*, meaning cap of happiness or good luck. We could not imagine any misfortune befalling a child born with a caul.

There was great rejoicing when we brought him home shortly after Christmas. He was a beautiful baby, with large blue eyes and lovely pale skin. He looked like his mother and his sister, Deirdre. He was a very quiet baby. One of my memories is how much I liked holding him at Mass on Sundays dressed in a white woollen jump suit, as he quietly stared at the nearest Mass-goers. I felt so proud holding such a handsome child.

Our quiet baby changed dramatically when he began to walk. Like most children, and particularly boys, he was fast on his feet, as wild as I was when I was a child – almost an extension of myself. He was full of curiosity, and seemed to have a hundred hands, all of them busily engaged! He was a witty child. From an early age he liked to dress up in funny clothes, and was very creative. This creativity turned to writing little stories by the time he was ten or eleven. He loved to write about ghosts and monsters. I discovered a great number of these after he died. As a young child he also wrote poetry; some of it, perhaps, prophetic. One of these was called 'The Seed' and I quote it verbatim:

> There once was a seed who didn't want to grow
> He wanted to stay in the dark down below.
> His brother's and sisters were growing up fast,
> They said hurry up brother or elss you'll be last.
> There brother said I am not growing up in the wind
>   and the rain
> I'll just stay here on my own to be soking and blowing
> I'll just stay here on my own.
> But his brothers and sisters said come brother grow.
> There brother said if you don't grow
> You'll never blow.

As he grew older this beautiful baby became a very handsome boy with lovely hair and a gentle smile. Our children remember him in different ways. He was Breda's favourite, and he nicknamed her 'the little red hen'. In her journal of 30 March 1991, a year after he was killed, she describes him as 'a lovable, innocent beautiful, funny child'. That really sums him up. She created a lovely portrait of him, and how they related:

> We would cycle to town together & I would buy him loads of sweets or a burger, chips & coke. It used to make me so happy to see his little face light up with delight. My brother appreciated everything. He was so vain, all done up in his jeans, runners & heavy metal t-shirt. His hair would have to be immaculate. If one hair

stood up it would be down to the bathroom for a quick splash in the sink, & then off to town to play computer games in the chipper or meet a few friends; a regular kid, but a special one. I used to say to him 'wait until you're old enough to go out with me, Cathal, we'll have a laugh, you and I' ...

I know that we are fortunate to have this lovely portrait of our youngest child, because today Breda might be unable to bring herself to recall him in such detail. One of the questions I asked my family was how they experienced Cathal from the time of his birth until he died. What type of personality came across to them? What were the things they most remembered about him? What were the things he did? How did he relate to them? How did they relate to him? They found this a very difficult exercise. It wasn't that we each did not have our own description of him, but that it forced us to bring him back to life. The soft-spoken, flesh and blood child. Not all members of my family were able to do it, and this is a barometer of how difficult and painful it is to lose a child or a sibling. However, we all grieve differently, and I know parents who get consolation from recalling their dead child in detail.

I still find it painful to remember him as the witty, funny child that he was. But, as part of writing this book, looking at photographs of him dressed up in his funny suits has helped me. I can smile when I remember how he used to call me 'Shiner', because of my bald head. It would have been a good nickname at school, but 'Jimmy' seemed to be what the boys preferred! This funny little boy also liked to take risks. I remember meeting him in the yard at 8 o'clock one summer morning. I assumed that he had got up early, and was out enjoying the sunshine. Only later did I learn that he and one of his friends had spent the night in an old, and apparently haunted, castle some distance from our house. I can also smile when I remember how his nephew, Gerald, adored him, and how Cathal used to tear around the house with Gerald gleefully hanging on in a wheelbarrow. The same pattern is now repeated with my very young grandchildren looking up to the older ones. I am aware of this with a mixture of joy and sadness. It reminds me of how Gerald must have felt bereaved when Cathal died. Although very young, he often asked where Cathal was. Bereavement psychologists remind us that children as young as two-and-a-half mourn.

Deirdre, too, shares her memories of Cathal, and brings him to life in a lovely, intimate way:

Cathal had a very bubbly personality. I always remember him as being happy and carefree. He loved life, living, animals, playing and music. And he really loved Dotty [our cocker spaniel]. We used to watch 'Home and Away' together, take off our socks and let Dotty lick our toes. There was nearly a fight over whose toes Dotty would lick. We all adored him. I was six years older and we spoiled him rotten. He was the centre of attention in our house. He had a wild streak, and loved dressing up when he was young. Gerald followed him around like a lapdog ...

We were teenagers at the time of his death. We had a typical brother/sister relationship, only we would have felt very protective of Cathal due to the age gap. I remember him turning green when he smoked Grandad's pipe. We used to dread him climbing and jumping off the walls when he was small. He had so much energy all of the time, and he always seemed so happy. He was game to try anything. He had no fears. He had a wonderful temperament.

He used to sleep with Breda in our bedroom. He was very close to her. She was so great at making up stories at nighttime. Her imagination was unbelievable. He was really into heavy metal music. Dad hated the t-shirts he wore. He grew so tall and was so handsome. I remember Dad used to get frustrated at him over his homework. He certainly wasn't a lover of books. He believed in happiness and having fun. He loved his bike and his radio/cassette player. He used to carry it around on the bike.

Deirdre is right. I worried a great deal about Cathal. I used to frustrate Mary talking about my worries when we went walking some evenings. I had a fear of heavy metal music, and all that it suggested to my conservative mind. I don't remember much of Cathal's primary school years. As with all our children, Mary helped him with his homework, and his time at school was uneventful. Each evening he liked to tell what had happened during the day. Indeed, most of our time was spent talking about school, which was tiresome for Mary.

I took a greater interest in his education when he entered the Christian Brothers Secondary School, Thurles, in September 1989, and since my colleagues never mentioned anything to me I assumed that he was coping well. He was an outdoor child and, as Deirdre said, wasn't keen on school. But, although wild, he was a very gentle child and never complained, so I was unaware that he was not making much progress. He found it hard to concentrate, and later I found out that he liked to entertain his friends in class by standing on the desk when the teachers were writing on the blackboard!

He must have been relieved when the first term ended, and looked forward to the Christmas holidays. As the youngest child, Christmas was a magical time for him. He loved helping me with the Christmas tree, and took delight in seeing the lights being turned on and the decorations going up throughout the house. He brought us a lovely fruit bowl,

and had hidden it for some time anticipating the childish pleasure of giving it to us on Christmas morning. It must have taken him a long time to save for it from the meagre pocket money that he had. We still have it, and for many years after his death it still held our fruit, but now sits in our sitting-room cabinet.

Cathal's lack of progress at secondary school became apparent when his first report arrived in January. I was worried and annoyed because I saw education as a means to freedom and autonomy. I think my children felt that I overemphasised education; but I came from an era and an area which saw few children go to secondary school. I feel so lucky and so grateful that my father sent me to secondary school. It changed my life, and I was determined that my children would make full use of secondary education.

Cathal's poor report resulted in some serious talking, and from what I could see he began to make a great effort. The comments by teachers at the first parent–teacher meeting in January 1990 were very favourable, and we were relieved and happy that he had settled down and was studying reasonably hard. We looked forward to the mid-term break in February.

CHAPTER TWO

Foreboding

A Premonition of Disaster

UNUSUALLY, PERHAPS, February was a sunny month. On Saturday 17th Mary and I decided that we would spend a day in Dublin, strolling around, enjoying the crowds, going into the shops, having coffee and lunch. We took the trip on the bus. It was very enjoyable as we sped along, and the green fields and the grazing animals spread out in a never-ending panorama.

We anticipated a pleasant day. But, as we entered the city centre my head began to pound. I never suffered from headaches, but this was totally debilitating. My head was pounding so much that I was unable to walk very far. We went into a cafe and sat there for an hour or so having coffee. I tried to resume our walk down Henry Street, but was unable. I spent the entire day in cafes, drinking coffee and feeling unaccountably depressed. I looked forward to the departure time for the bus, and gradually as we made our way home the pain eased.

Only months later, when we were talking about that day in Dublin, did I connect it to the affliction that was about to visit our family the following day. My daughter, Breda, had a much more startling experience beginning on Friday 16th. She was living in London at the time, and planned an early night in bed having had a busy week at work. Her entry in her diary explains what happened:

I went to bed & for some reason I couldn't sleep & started to have an odd feeling that something bad was going to happen. I tossed & turned & eventually gave up & lay on my back when suddenly something caught my eye, & looking up at the light (which was off) I could clearly see a bright crystal-like object, white strands of light joined together haphazardly in no particular form or shape, moving strands, yet not moving from the position over the lampshade. Normally I would have been frightened & would have jumped out of bed & ran for the nearest person, but I felt peaceful & went to sleep almost immediately.

Breda's apprehension returned on Saturday, the day Mary and I were in Dublin. She wrote that she was feeling quite ill and had 'a foreboding feeling that something was about to happen ...'

The next day Breda went to South Harrow to visit my beloved aunt Nell. She felt depressed and talked to Nell about Cathal, how poor his school report had been, how she worried that he was 'so wild' and that his dad 'might come down hard on him'. Nell urged her to ring home, but Breda felt unable to do so, feeling that there was 'something awful after happening'. She felt very close to her uncle Tom, Mary's brother, and 'for some strange reason' she wanted to hear his voice, and so went to his house. Breda noted that 'our conversation was mostly about Cathal. Cathal & I were very close & very alike in ways that only we knew ...'

Breda felt better after talking to Tom and went to her flat where she had a similar conversation with her flatmate, who reassured her that Cathal would be all right. In the midst of that reassurance the phone rang.

CHAPTER THREE

Death Comes Amongst Us

When Time Stood Still in the Shadow of Death

SUNDAY 18 FEBRUARY 1990 will forever be indelibly imprinted on my mind. It was a beautiful day, and better still we were on mid-term break. In those days I had a particular routine on Sundays. I always went to 11 o'clock Mass, followed by lunch. I frequently visited relations, sometimes went for a drive, or othertimes spent the afternoon reading the paper and dozing. That day, instead of going for a drive, Mary and I went for a short walk after lunch. We passed Cathal and one of his friends, P.J., chatting by the bridge. The bridge spanned a small stream, which flowed gently along the bottom of our lawn, and was like a magnet for all the children around. We stopped for a few words with the boys, and continued our leisurely stroll. I did not know that I would never speak with my child again.

When I was sorting the material relating to Cathal for this book, I found a tear-stained note written by Mary looking back on that Sunday:

> My last words to Cathal on the Sunday he died were, 'Cathal, you don't talk much to your Mam'. He just laughed at me and went off on his bike. That morning he had left a little note on the table saying he was going to Mass with us. Little did I think that that was his last

Sunday at Mass with us. If we only had gone visiting, things might be different today.

After lunch I lay on the couch and read the paper, alternating between reading and dozing. It was so peaceful and relaxing. The world was a friendly and safe place. Then at 3.50 p.m. the doorbell rang. It continued to ring shrilly, urgently, persistently. I opened the door to find Alan, another of Cathal's friends, there, terror in his eyes. His words are still clear in my mind: 'There's been a terrible accident,' he stammered. He did not say who was in the accident and it never crossed my mind that my child was the victim. I went to the road to see what I could do, and saw Cathal lying there, as if he was asleep. There was no blood, and I assumed that he was unconsciousness and would soon wake up. It was incomprehensible that my child had been fatally injured. The thought never crossed my mind. Mary, on the other hand, kept saying, 'Cathal is going to die, Cathal is going to die'. I felt irritated with her and said, 'Of course he's not going to die'. I felt no panic because I did not think that he was badly injured. Perhaps I blocked out such an unimaginable thought.

I never noticed his mangled bicycle, or the deep dent in the roof of the car, which struck him as he emerged from a side road. I wasn't in shock, but felt helpless. The sister of the driver of the car asked to use the phone to contact their parents, and I felt a surge of rage at this for no apparent reason. My main concern was to see that Cathal was kept warm, so we got a blanket and covered him until the ambulance arrived. I examined the face of the nurse, who was our neighbour, for reassurance, but could see none. Still the incomprehensible had not registered with me. Mary and I followed the ambulance to the hospital in Cashel. I had changed my VHI policy some time earlier, and was unsure of Cathal's cover. I worried that I would be presented with a large bill for his stay in hospital, and hoped it would only be for a few days.

When we arrived at the hospital, the ambulance driver was outside the door smoking a cigarette. Wisps of smoke curled slowly upwards and vanished into the air. He looked serious, and I merely assumed that he was an unfriendly person. I wondered aloud when I would hear that Cathal had recovered con-sciousness. The driver's gloomy face and lack of response to my statement made me uneasy. Even then I failed to realise that Cathal had been seriously injured. When I entered the hospital I met a nurse who told us to 'pray hard'. This shocked me, and for the first time I began to recognise that my youngest child was in a serious condition. But I still could not comprehend it. How could I contemplate that my son might die! I was in total ignorance of what it was like to be bereaved. I had never experienced the death of anyone close to me. I am an only child, and my parents were then in their early seventies. How could such a thing happen to me? I dismissed the thought and awaited my child to regain consciousness, and then all would be well again. Perhaps he might have broken a leg, and would miss some school. Even the thought that he might have suffered brain damage never occured to me. Yes! A broken leg, at most.

Bill was the only member of our family with us. Our kind neighbours, David and Eileen, (who were the parents of P.J., Cathal's close friend, who had been with him until shortly before the accident) had travelled to the hospital hoping, like myself, that Cathal would recover. They met Bill and his girlfriend walking on the road, and brought them to the hospital.

The surgeon soon arrived. He was dressed in long leather boots, and had obviously been out riding or hunting. And then, twenty minutes later, the nurse came out and said, 'I'm sorry, we could not save him'. It was only when I read the inquest report as part of the research for this book did I realise that Cathal could not have survived, and that no doctor could have saved him. The poor child suffered extensive fractures to his skull and bleeding to his brain.

I immediately understood the reality: death had come to my family. I was not hysterical, but felt a numbing sense of shock. I climbed the steps of the hospital in a daze, and was unaware of anyone else around me. Then I heard Mary screaming. The staff did not want her to go into the room where Cathal lay. I could sense her anger as she pushed them aside. I stumbled after her. We stood beside the narrow bed and stared down uncomprehendingly at our child. I began to experience that dead feeling within me. Cathal looked so peaceful at the beginning of his eternal sleep. I stroked his hair, just as I had often stroked it when he was asleep in his room at home. I often wondered then if he knew I was there, and was pretending to be asleep on those occasions. As he lay in the hospital his hair was so soft, and his skin was warm. This added to the unreality. Bill was with us in that small room. For him it was 'just chaos, a blur. I vaguely remember it not being real'.

Strangely, at this moment of awful pain I felt my faith and my spirituality coming to the surface in a powerful, unexpected surge. I began to pray silently, and I remember clearly the words I used: 'Jesus, I offer you my child.' I could see a timber cross, and I could feel it crashing down on my shoulders. I felt my body buckle beneath its weight, but for whatever reason, I felt comfort in the midst of the shock and pain. I had always been a spiritual and religious person, but in these years had become rather apathetic and indifferent. Now I was experiencing a powerful religious and spiritual feeling. This was my individual experience, but I have to say that the comfort did not last for very long.

Cathal's sisters would have to be told. Someone rang Tom to contact Breda, and when her phone rang her sense of

foreboding had now passed, and she cheerfully greeted Tom.
I don't know who contacted him, but having heard the bad
news he worked out how he would tell her. 'Breda, I've got
some very bad news for you', was the simple, quiet address.
Breda recorded the panic and fear she felt at those words:

> My stomach immediately knotted, I panicked, it had
> happened – that something that was in the back of my
> head. Inside I was screaming, 'Please God, not my
> mother', outwardly saying, 'Tom, don't tell me, I don't
> want to know, I'll go crazy'. He said he'd pick me up at
> Northolt tube station. I hung up & went into my
> flatmate, I was out of control. 'My mother is dead; I
> know she is, what will I do?' Oh God!

Somehow Breda got a taxi, and headed for Northolt station.
She doesn't remember paying the driver as she got out. Tom
was already at the station and she rushed towards him, 'but
hoping that I'd never get there'. Tom hugged her and said,
'Darling, you must be very brave. Be strong for me; you
promise?' Breda continues in her diary:

> I was bewildered, confused, irrational. 'It's my Mam,
> she's dead, isn't she?' 'No darling, she's not dead,' he
> said. 'It's my dad then, he's dead' (I was always afraid my
> father would die before I told him I loved him). 'No, it's
> not your dad.' 'Then who? Deirdre? Frances? It's Fran
> isn't it?' Pictures of her being stabbed somewhere in
> New York were floating through my mind. I was going
> totally crazy. 'Breda, it's Cathal.' 'No, no, he's hurt, oh
> God, what happened?' No reaction from Tom. Cold
> realisation. 'He's dead. Tell me he's not, Tom, please.'

When Tom explained that Cathal had been killed in a road

accident Breda screamed, and went into shock, which she described as being cocooned in 'subconscious protective cotton wool'. Breda's cotton wool image would not describe the violent sense of shock that Bill or I felt. For me it was like a shotgun blast in my face, leaving a heavy grey cloud suffocating me and closing down my senses. For Bill it was like being kicked violently in the face by a 'size twelve, steel toe-capped boot … it is as though some force has reached into your brain and unplugged it'. Apart from that, Bill describes the memory of how he reacted as 'blurry':

> I could not process what I was told. Tried to understand it, but it simply did not register with me. I remember being more impacted by how upset David was, and trying to understand how serious this was. I recall trying to figure out what I should do next. It did not hit me. I was confused.

He remembers, however, the sense of disbelief that gripped him:

> The unbelievable had happened. My brother had been tragically killed at the young age of thirteen. What the hell is going on? … People consoled me. What the hell is going on? … People crushed me. What the hell is going on? My family, once a happy lot, are shattered … what the hell is going on? My friends can barely look me in the eye. What the hell is going on?

Mary, Bill and I seemed to have been sitting in the small room for an eternity. A nurse eventually came and gave us sweet tea to allay the shock. I was utterly dazed, but somehow in my befuddled state of mind I knew that Frances and Deirdre would have to be contacted. My mind and sense of competence were rapidly closing down as the reality of what had happened sunk in. I was unable to give any thought as to how I would prepare Frances and Deirdre for this news. I simply said that I would ring them, and must have sounded quite normal to those around me as I explained this. The nurse led me to a telephone, and I rang Deirdre first, telling her the news without any preparation. I could hear her screams echoing down the phone line. She was in Killoran, a townland only a few miles from our house, with Denis, her boyfriend, now her husband. They were in a pleasant domestic setting, sitting down to tea with Denis's mother, Nan, and other visiting members of the family. Deirdre vividly described her reactions when I rang:

> My immediate reaction was to scream hysterically. I felt disbelief – this can't be happening; it's only a dream; I had misheard Dad. I felt huge panic. I remember screaming repeatedly, and Nan coming to me, holding me very tightly. I remember doing my level best to escape from her grip, to run out of the house and get home. I recall kicking and lashing out at Nan in order to get free. I recall Denis's aunt saying that they would have to give me something to calm me down.

Deirdre's screams unnerved me. I retreated further into a world of darkness. In a robot-like fashion I grappled with how I would contact Frances who was working at the famous Pete's Tavern in New York City. I must have seemed not only normal but composed and efficient to those who observed me contacting the telephone exchange. I remember calmly telling the operator that my son had been killed, and that I needed to contact my daughter in Pete's Tavern, New York. He quickly got me the number, and I dialled and asked for Frances. I was so overwhelmed that I did not think of asking for the manager to break the news to her. When she came to

the phone I was barely able to stammer out the fateful words
that her brother had been killed. I heard her scream and then
the line seemed to go dead. I cannot remember what
happened as I stood there with the silent phone in my hand,
but Frances takes up the story of how the horror overwhelmed
her when she got my call:

> It seemed like any ordinary Sunday. Business was fairly
> slow. We were laughing and joking around ... One of my
> co-workers told me that I had a phone call. My blood
> ran cold. Somehow I knew it was bad news. My Dad was
> on the phone, his voice distraught & cracked. Without
> any preamble he said, 'Frances, Cathal was killed today'.
> Everything stood still. My head spun. I dropped the
> phone, ran into the back and collapsed. I didn't come to
> for a few minutes. I don't remember how I communicated
> the news. I remember feeling compelled to get home as
> soon as physically possible. That became my sole focus.

I feel so sad when I consider how bluntly Frances and Deirdre
were told of their brother's death. I was in no state to prepare
them for the news, nor indeed was I in any state to have made
such sensitive and traumatic phone calls. These calls should
have been made by someone else, and Denis and the Tavern's
manager should have been contacted first, to ensure that some
support was in place for my two daughters.

Frances needed as much emotional support as she could
get when confronted with this unexpected and ghastly news.
Unfortunately, such support was not forthcoming:

> My boyfriend & I left work to get the next flight out. We
> had just enough money for the cab fare to the airport,
> and a one way ticket. I desperately wanted him to come
> with me. I didn't know how I would do this alone. He

rationally explained that one of us had to earn money for rent. I didn't want logic. I wanted a love that would walk me through the worst time of my life, then and since. I remember thinking that I would never allow him to face something like this alone, no matter the cost. It was the death knell of our relationship.

I have no memory of our co-workers' reactions.

By that stage I was overwhelmed. I could not bear to hear the screaming and pain of my surviving children. I felt the energy leaving my body after telling Frances; I felt myself further retreating into a world of helplessness. I had always been seen by my family as a competent go-getter; a person who decided what he wanted to do, and went ahead and did it. I was seen by them as a great achiever. Bill was especially conscious about how I had been, and how I was that night:

> My father was shattered. He was a rock of strength – a harsh father but a rock – and here he is devastated. This did not make sense. This is my most lasting memory.

I became so distraught that I was unable to make even the simplest decision. Making further phone calls was too much for me. Somebody else would have to make the appropriate arrangements for Cathal's funeral. I could not even think of the fundamentals, such as getting a grave. Little did I think that I would need a grave for any of my family. Somebody else would have to do it. Bill had more recollection and more strength than I had. In the midst of his pain and mental chaos he, and his uncle Tim, set about getting a grave. Bill, in fact, picked out three graves together '... for Cathal, Mam & Dad – imagine that! I often wondered after that how I thought so clearly.'

My shocked family had to struggle through that afternoon

and evening, when time lost all meaning for us. Deirdre, having heard the bad news, could not, and cannot to this day, recollect leaving Denis's house and getting to Cashel hospital. All she can recall is 'a constant feeling of extreme numbness'. Mary and I waited in the small room for Deirdre to come. Bill was so upset that he would not go in to see Cathal, but was with us in the waiting room when she arrived. Deirdre felt as if it was an eternity before she was allowed in to see her brother. She recalled how upset Mary was, but apart from that she felt frozen, 'as if I was no longer in control of my own body, as if I was not really physically present, but in another place'.

When she was allowed in to see Cathal, she stumbled into the little room where he was laid out and I can remember her horror-struck face when she saw her brother on the bed. I felt so helpless. I wanted to support my children, but I was unable to support even myself. I had mentally, but not emotionally, accepted that Cathal was dead. Deirdre could not accept this reality, especially as her brother looked as if he was asleep. This is the image that stuck in her mind:

> When I saw Cathal in the hospital I began to believe that he was only sleeping. He looked so peaceful, looked the same as he always did. I really began to think that he would most definitely wake up any minute, that he would move, even a small movement to show us that he would live. I felt very strongly that he wasn't dead, that he would come home, and that the doctors were wrong.

Meanwhile in London, Tom, knowing that he could not protect Breda from the pain of grief, was doing everything in his power to console and support her, and help her find her way home to rejoin her shattered family. She recorded those moments in her diary:

I packed my case, pulling out my black clothes with a macabre logic. Tom drove me to his house, where his wife, Vourneen, put her arms around me, and made me a hot whiskey. By now I was in a complete state of shock, completely and utterly oblivious to the painful reality, my mind was numb ... I vaguely remember ringing my work associate & friend Katie & telling her calmly why I wouldn't be in for a while. I remember trying to estimate for her how long I would be gone, as if I was going to a wedding. Totally unreal.

Tom put me on a 9 o'clock plane to Dublin. Time lost all meaning. I first had to get there, but inside my mind was in turmoil. I was almost wondering, 'why am I going home'. My uncle Tim and his wife, Mary, met me, but I was feeling mentally & physically drained & hardly functioning. I had only a deep sense of nothingness.

Frances had a much longer flight to make. I cannot imagine what that seven-hour trip must have been like for her. She attempts to describe it:

The flight home was totally surreal. I could not process the reality of this truth I had been delivered. This happened to other vague people somewhere dimly out there. Their pain never impinged on our world, never mind a tragedy like theirs. The horror that it might be true was under the surface for the entire flight. I had to see his dead body to believe. Nothing less would persuade me.

I remember nothing about the journey from the airport home, not even who drove. I remember nothing about meeting my family, or entering the house. I was consumed by the need to see Cathal. It was like a force driving me forward.

CHAPTER FOUR

Helplessness and Horror

A Family Sinking into Darkness and Chaos

A S BREDA AND Frances made their way back to Ireland to confront this dark spectre of death, the rest of our family sat disconsolately in the small waiting room of the hospital, until we summoned the energy to leave. Darkness had fallen when we began to make our way home. Neither moon nor stars were shining that night. Our neighbours had remained with us in the waiting room as we sat in dazed silence. What was there to say? We were still in shock and disbelief. What was this all about? Chaos! A world destroyed! Survival! Helplessness! And ultimately, horror. I cannot remember if I drove home. Probably not. But, I do remember the darkness as we came into the yard of our house. It is one of the clearest and bleakest memories I have. With my senses heightened, I became conscious of the house being shrouded in a deep gloom of blackness. What had once been a warm and welcoming home was now a cold building brooding under a winter sky. The heat was not on, and the house was freezing. I felt at that time that this house would never be the same again. I felt that laughter and fun would never be heard there anymore. And so it was for a long time.

That evening at home was a prolonged nightmare. Time ceased for me. I lay on a couch beside the fire, and was barely aware of people calling to sympathise with us. I could not respond emotionally to them. I'm sure I replied politely to their kindness, but I was feeling dead on the inside. Totally devastated.

Bill was in a 'chaotic' state of mind, trying to make some sense of it all:

> This was not supposed to happen. Normality was gone. How could we recover from this? Confusion. What was I supposed to do? Tired. Exhausted. Wanted to sleep.

But, he was unable to sleep. Deirdre, still in a daze, 'couldn't tell what was going on around me. I remember lying on the sitting room carpet with Denis that night, being exhausted, but unable to sleep or rest'. We all awaited the arrival of Breda with dread and apprehension. Our family was slowly getting together in a context never before experienced.

Now with her uncle Tim and his wife, Mary, Breda's sense of numbness ebbed and flowed: 'the horror came floating back.' Her aunt Breda was there and Breda implored her aunt to assure her that it wasn't true. She fluctuated between numbness, anguish, denial and anger. It seemed as if the world had gone mad, that her relatives had gone mad. She rang her mother and thought that she sounded tired. She was ambiguous about getting home and facing the nightmare; she had a strong desire to be with her family and an equally strong wish that she would never reach home. As she stood in Tim's sitting room, she felt a great rage, particularly at God: 'I felt like smashing all the windows, kicking down the doors. I wanted to scream "f–k you God, you b——d. I hate you".' I was to experience such anger much later.

Tim drove Breda home. She was comforted by her aunt, Breda, whom we regarded almost as our own daughter. They drove slowly into our yard, and when she got out, Bill and

Deirdre embraced her, drawing comfort from each other. The remainder of her diary entry on that night shows how a family can cling together in the face of adversity, and try to support each other. It also shows how children (in this case some of them adult children) are conscious of the loss of support from their parents, who are themselves trying to survive. This adds to their fear and their pain:

By the time I got home I was numb again. 3 a.m. & there's voices everywhere. I couldn't believe it – the sitting room full of people I hardly recognised. I just saw my father, like I've never seen him, sitting hunched in the armchair, shattered. He got up & grabbed hold of me, sobbing. He sounded like he was in physical pain. 'Poor Breda, you loved him, he was your pet, he loved you.' I remember telling him it would be alright; I was embarrassed for him. I hadn't grasped the reality of it all, but seeing my Dad so vulnerable & weak tore me apart. He was the rock our family depended on; whenever I was sick, even now, I would go to him first before anybody, & he always helped & knew what to do, & here he was crumbling & saying, 'Breda, I've always been able to help ye before, but this time I can't. I'm finished. My beautiful son'. We stood there for hours, or so it seemed, me incapable of any kind of feeling. Then I went to look for my mother. She was in bed, pale & lifeless. She could barely talk, & when she cried my heart was breaking ...

Deirdre & her boyfriend, Denis, me & my aunt Margaret stayed up all night because we were to collect Frances from Shannon the following morning. We just sat & cried all night. The night passed slowly, everyone locked in their own thoughts, my aunt Margaret struggling to keep a brave face in front of us all. Tim was sleeping in the bed my darling brother had slept & dreamt in a few hours before.

As we passed the night encased in our own nightmare, comforted by friends and relatives, Frances was making her long trip home. I went to bed in the early hours of the morning, and, after a few hours' deep sleep, awoke very early to the nightmare. It was crushing. As I gathered my confused thoughts, denial and incomprehension returned. As the cold reality of what had happened sank in I felt terror. I had never experienced anything like it before. I cannot describe what terror really is. It manifested itself as a knot in my stomach. A feeling of panic. I felt physically sick, wretched and helpless. How could my child be dead? This cannot have happened! Why was I not able to prevent it? Surely I should have been able to do something to prevent this? Never did I feel so disabled. I realise as I write this that I cannot find the words to express how I felt on that first morning after Cathal's death. The numbness was gone, and the horror fully felt.

Mary lay silent beside me, struck dumb by the horror of losing one of her children. Unspeaking, and feeling the unimaginable. She is a gentle person with a great love for her children. She was always there to greet them when they came home from school. The dinner was always ready. They usually had some story for her about what had happened that day. I had not as yet begun to worry about how she would cope with this. I was hardly able to cope myself. But any injury to any of her children caused her alarm and worry. Now one of them was dead. Our youngest child, and therefore the one who needed most care, was gone. Mothers begin to bond with their unborn child shortly after conception. It is a most powerful bond. Death does not destroy it. It remains as strong as ever. This made Mary's loss more poignant and sad.

I became even more aware of this bond and this maternal love from a book that I am currently reading entitled *Behind the Lines* by Andrew Carroll. It is a book which quotes the letters of various people written during the major wars waged since the eighteenth century. One of these was written by a Hungarian doctor, Anna Koppich, whose young son perished in Auschwitz-Birkenau concentration camp, where she, too, was imprisoned. I was moved by the following lines:

> And now I have a confession to make. For many, many years, even after I gave birth, I thought that being in love is the most formidable, the strongest feeling in the world. Later I realised, however, what being a mother means. I found out that motherly love is way above any other kind, a kind of love that is so little talked about, so little written about.

But these were not my thoughts on that morning. They would come later, and cause me worry and anxiety. For now I had to survive. There was no question of my being the big strong father. There could be no pretence here. This was real. There was no hiding this vulnerability. But, vulnerability is our greatest strength. It causes us to reach out for help. But who would I reach out to? I did not have the strenght to reach out. All those in the house could not support me. I dragged myself out of bed and made some tea. I cannot recall if the others were up. I don't suppose we had much to say, except to sit morosely, and dwell in our sad thoughts.

Breda and her aunt Margaret had long gone to Shannon Airport to collect Frances. What an unenviable errand! Breda describes what it was like for them:

> Our journey to Shannon was a nightmare; bitter stormy weather, to match our emotions. Meeting Fran had

broken my barriers temporarily, & the raw pain made me feel so ill, & the anger boiled within me. I was afraid of the love we shared in my family, the feeling of togetherness we had. It scared me. I wished we hadn't been so close, it wasn't worth it. I hated God. My family never did anything to deliberately hurt anyone, & he had rewarded us by snatching away the child we adored & idolised. I felt myself drift in & out of sanity, hardly aware of what went on, bouts of numbness interrupted by sharp stabs of physical pain in my stomach. I wanted to go to Cathal & wrap my arms around him like before & tell him it would be okay. I was so angry that God hadn't taken me instead.

That day the nightmare intensified. I was called to go to the hospital and identify Cathal in the morgue. Frances, Breda and Bill wished to come and support me. Frances, who was exhausted from the journey home from the United States and from the trauma, has the clearest description of what it was like for Bill and herself:

I remember that Dad was to identify the body at the morgue of Cashel Hospital. As I had been many times before, I was once again his companion in the hard moments. Bill came too. Cathal was unmistakeably dead. In those days, undertakers took no pains to conceal death. His yellow pallor was the ultimate proof. He always had a rosy, healthy complexion. I've come to associate that waxy, yellow colour with death.

Bill entered for just a second and went around the side to vomit repeatedly. We were broken.

Our lives had stopped. I remember resenting every laugh I heard, every sign of life. I wanted to scream, 'How can you laugh and joke? Don't you know what has happened?' I couldn't understand why everyone didn't feel the cataclysm. I was enraged that some seismic scale hadn't registered it to the world.

Breda wanted to be near Cathal, 'to touch him, to stay with him; the urgent need to do this was choking me'. But, the ordeal of seeing him for the first time was too much for her:

> When we arrived I couldn't do it, I couldn't look at him. I didn't want to see his body I loved so much bruised & bloody. I'd rather die. It would have haunted me forever. If only I could have talked to him; even if he had lived & been in a vegetative state I could have gone back home & minded him.

I can well understand why Breda did not wish to enter that morgue, and I am glad that she did not do so. I can understand how appalled Frances was, and how Bill could be so physically ill. Of all the experiences of that first week, and of the entire grieving process, this was the most painful one for me. I watch the *Silent Witness* drama on television quite frequently, and most episodes include morgue scenes. Pulling back the sheet to reveal the naked corpse is just a moment of drama, which most people barely notice. But for me this now evokes memories of that terrible day. I was led into the morgue in Cashel by the late Inspector Ned Lafferty. Ned, whom I got to know much later when I was the principal of Our Lady's Secondary School, showed himself to be a warm, generous and caring person that day.

I watched immobilised by horror as they pulled back the sheet that covered Cathal. I hardly recognised my child. When I had seen him on the previous day in the hospital he had been warm, his soft hair resting lightly on the pillow. Now I saw this pale corpse, his head bandaged, in this cold place. I could see the great black marks on his shoulders and his side, showing that he had tried to turn away from the car when he had rounded the corner and crossed the road. This memory is the one that reminds me of his last seconds, as I cycle by that place every day. I felt his forehead, and now I understood what the coldness of death really meant. It was an icy coldness that somehow sapped the humanness from my child.

Ned Lafferty led me from that place, a warm figure trying to negate the coldness I had experienced. My legs could just about carry me as I emerged, crushed, from the morgue. I walked robot-like to complete the formalities of the post-mortem, and I still feel angry at what followed. I am still conscious of the formality of that interview with the pathologist who asked me various questions for his records. Did he not realise that I was traumatised? Could he not have summoned some brief expression of sympathy even if he did not mean it? Of course, I realise that doctors cannot allow themselves to be subject to the sadness they witness every day. It would be overwhelming and non-productive. But surely some small expression of sympathy, some acknowledgement of the pain experienced by the individual, would not be too much to ask for. It would have made it easier for me as I answered his questions about Cathal. At a three-day seminar on bereavement in Ballinasloe some years afterwards, I met other bereaved people who felt as I did. I really hope that nowadays the human element as well as the professional is considered in the training of medical people.

I drove home that day, Monday 19 February, full of misery and anger, but I think that the horror of that entire experience either anaesthetised me for the demands of the funeral, or else it made everything that followed less overwhelming. That evening we had to return, as a family, to the funeral room attached to the hospital. For a time I grew to hate that hospital because of the bad memories it held for me. Our small family tried to console each other and pray together as we stood beside the coffin, before the public arrived to offer their sympathy.

I sensed the fear and the pain of my family as we entered the funeral room, which was beside the morgue. Having experienced the coldness and bareness of the morgue there was some comfort for me that the funeral room, while sparse, was at least warm. For some of my family it was different. They had not yet seen Cathal after the post-mortem, and were unprepared for the trauma of seeing him laid out in a coffin. There is something unnatural about seeing a child lying in a coffin. I cannot imagine the trauma suffered by Mary at seeing Cathal that evening, and I did not distress her by asking as I write this book. She still finds it very painful to talk about the events of those days. All I remember is wishing that he was buried and that it all might go away. I envy people who have their deceased children laid out in their own homes. They seem to get relief from the pain. It is like holding on to their children for as long as possible. But, I could not bear to do this, and Mary recently told me that she felt the same.

For Bill, seeing Cathal in the coffin was 'hell'. He screamed and ran away, but I made him return and see the corpse of his brother, knowing, in my less confused state of mind, that it would be a cause of regret to him if he did not do so. I sensed then what I know now: that it is important to experience as much of the pain as possible immediately after a death, and that it is particularly important to see the body of the deceased. It brings home the reality of the loss and is essential for proper healing. Failure to do this, or, as sometimes happens, being numbed by tablets, can prolong the grieving process and lead to complicated grieving. Bill confirms how seeing Cathal's body brought the reality of the death into focus. 'I was devastated,' he wrote. 'I think this was the first time it hit me ... the worst moment of my life to date.' Deirdre also confirms how the distressing reality then began to take hold:

> The funeral home was the most horrendous of all. It was then that it hit me very hard that Cathal was not coming back to us. He was lying in his uniform in the white coffin, and I knew for certain that he was gone from us for good, that there was no way we could get him back. I felt immense grief and sadness. I remember the black marks on his fingers from the accident. I recall how white he was ... and all of us crying uncontrollably.

Breda's account recorded at the time shows the trauma of the family as we clung together, and how the numbness prevented her from crying:

> The coffin lay open ... I could see a bandage. I walked closer & saw what will always be the worst moment of my life: my brother Cathal, dead. I pictured him sleeping beside me in my bed, I would sit & look at his sweet innocent face ... this was different. He was white, colourless, his lips were bloodless but there was blood around his mouth, his tiny nose was bruised & his forehead a strange shape. But the worst of it was the bandage; they had shaved his beautiful hair off, the hair he was so proud of, which, despite all my dad's stern warnings, he refused to cut short.
>
> I touched him – his skin was shockingly cold, like marble; my brother, a cuddly, lively, warm little boy lying here like an empty shell. I traced his face, the face I loved, his eyelids, his forehead, lips, then his entwined fingers & bloodless hands. I didn't cry. I couldn't. I just needed to be with him. That's the only feeling I had.

Frances recollects how austere the hospital funeral home was:

> Cathal was not at a funeral home. He was in a very small stone building on the hospital grounds. The building in its austerity reminded me of a monk's cell. There was none of the comforts of a funeral home. And that seemed fitting to me. His body had filled out since I'd seen him the year before. I remember thinking that he would have been strong and broad like my uncles. The doctor told mammy how strong and well-cared for he looked. That broke us even more. The needlessness. The waste.
>
> We all stacked our hands on his chest. I don't remember whose hand went first. But each of us automatically planted one hand on the next. We were declaring our unity as a family that would always include Cathal. Somehow his chest felt hollow, as if it would cave away. I couldn't bear the signs that he had been hurt. The blood compacted in his nostrils, the massive bruising on his neck, behind his shirt collar, and, easily imagined, down his entire back.

----◆◆◆----

CHAPTER FIVE

Public Grief

*Family Distress as the Coffin Lid is Bolted and the Face
of our Child is Hidden Forever*

W E TOOK OUR seats and the doors were opened.
The death of a child is what bereavement
psychologists call a particularly enfranchised loss.
What that means is that it evokes widespread sympathy. And
so it was with us. A great number of people slowly made their
way into the room. It was very moving for me. Yet it was also
an ordeal. I was too devastated to really appreciate it until
many years had passed. I was trying to come to terms with
Cathal's death and meet all these people. Some friends of my
childhood came to sympathise, and I found this very
emotional. Somehow my own childhood and that of my lost
child became entangled in my mind, as I met those childhood
friends long unseen.

Other members of our family wanted all this precious time
with Cathal to be for the family only. Frances records that
she was

> hysterical, just hysterical. I resented every single person
> in that place that was not my immediate family. I felt
> this should have been for us only. He was ours and we
> needed that time alone with him. I wanted to tell them
> all to get out. I remember the insane comments people
> made by way of comfort to my mother: 'God needed him';

'he's a little angel now'; 'sure he didn't suffer.'

I could see that every comment cut my mother's soul. It was those who just cried with her that made any difference at all. One of my best friends didn't come to the funeral or the wake. She said by way of explanation that we were too emotional a family and she couldn't take the excess of grief she knew we would express.

It seemed like an eternity, but finally the long line of people passing by ceased and the door was closed. Our family were again alone with our child, and I felt the loneliness of losing Cathal increase in the silence before the final prayers. I listened sadly and incredulously to these prayers, and waited for the coffin to be closed.

I will never forget that moment. It was a potent reminder of this unwelcome reality. I felt physically sick as the lid was closed and stared in horror as the bolts tightened. I could feel my anguish and my fear increase as I got the last glimpse of my child. I felt so helpless. What could I do? How could I bring him back? Is this real? We were all thinking the same way. Insignificant humans, powerless to prevent death claiming our child. Death had taken him, and the grave would claim him. We could not prevent it. Breda wrote that she was mentally screaming, 'no way, I'm not going anywhere & neither is he. How did anybody think they could take away what was rightfully ours. He was our baby'. Deirdre also found this moment unbearable, and recalls 'wanting to stay with him all of the time, not wanting to be taken away from him. I remember the screams from all of us when they took Cathal away, and we had to leave'.

Frances, still hysterical, refused to budge:

When the undertaker came to take Cathal, I would not leave. I was outraged that he was being taken – our boy.

I wanted to be alone with him now that the public was gone. The other members of my family dutifully left when asked. But I stayed. I screamed something at the undertaker. My uncle Pat finally removed me.

Death took us by the hand, and we emerged from the funeral room, and slowly made our way through the large crowd. I remember the narrow path as people stood sombrely in a long line on either side. The hospital seemed to cast its huge shadow over us as we made our way to our cars. Slowly we followed the hearse the fifteen miles to the Cathedral of the Assumption in Thurles. The family were in the front car, still in disbelief that the body of their youngest member was being carried in a coffin to repose in front of the magnificent altar of the Cathedral. He was too young. This should not be.

The crowd that awaited us was enormous. The whole area around the Cathedral and the side streets were filled with cars. It was almost like a match day. I wondered what was going on in the town, and only slowly realised that this great crowd was waiting for us. We were swamped with people as we tried to make our way into the crammed Cathedral. The First and Sixth year students of Thurles Christian Brothers School formed a guard of honour as we made our way in, and a great body of students added to the huge crowd in the Cathedral. I felt greatly moved by the sea of grey uniforms. We made our way slowly up the main aisle, and took our place in the front seat, opposite the coffin.

How often had I seen bereaved families in that front seat, never realising that I would be there at such an early stage in my life. It was unbelievable. Again a long queue of people passed by sympathising. This is an important and necessary part of the funeral ritual, symbolising the support of the local community, and adding to the healing aspects of grief. Deirdre, however, cannot recall any of the funeral service. For her it 'was like an out-of-body experience, as if I wasn't really present'. Neither can Frances remember anything about that evening in the Cathedral. Bill was supported by his friends:

> They distracted me. I was not accepting it. It was like a break from reality. I actually laughed and joked some – which is very strange now that I look back. I remember not interacting much with my shattered family.

Mary was broken-hearted and overcome by the huge crowd, and Breda had a roller coaster of negative emotions as she struggled with the appalling reality that was so suddenly handed to her:

> We were swamped with people automatically shaking our hands. All the time I was feeling alone. I didn't need anybody's pity. I hated it, but I did wish my old boyfriend was there. I needed him, but I couldn't give in to that fact. I was determined to do it by myself.

Our dejected departure from the Cathedral did not bring much relief. We came home exhausted and withdrawn even from each other. There was not sufficient energy to sustain us, and we had to rely on our wider family for support. My brothers-in-law and sisters-in-law did the best they could, but they, too, were exhausted. I will always appreciate them for their kindness. They continued to visit us and be with us for a long time after Cathal's death. My own parents did not know what to do. As a young man, my father, who was the eldest in the family, lost his seventeen-year-old sister, two younger siblings and his mother when she was in her forties. He looked so sad and so helpless. I remember him saying to me that the pain would get less and less and eventually go away. Many years before, my parents-in-law had lost two children and no doubt were now coping with their own renewed grief. At that time I would have loved to have had brothers and sisters of my own; my own flesh and blood who might understand my pain. But who can understand the pain of a parent who has lost a child! It was a lonely time, and that loneliness continued for many years.

Breda's journal records what that evening was like for her:

> We drifted to bed, eventually exhausted, after nothing to eat, but not hungry at all. I lay in bed with Fran, in my bed that I had shared for years with Cathal. I knew that bed would be a terrible reminder from now on. We used to lie in bed & talk into the night, keeping my sister, Deirdre, awake. I told him everything about my boyfriends, boys I liked, etc. It seems stupid but despite his innocent ways he understood it all, & I knew that. Deirdre would scream at us to keep quiet, & both of us would have to climb under the bed clothes & smother our giggles. He would lie awake waiting for me to come in from a disco or from meeting my boyfriend.
>
> It was the hardest night of my life. I lay there thinking of the times I had fought with him over stupid things, like when he had broken my expensive jewellery box that some friends in Limerick had bought me. I was so angry; I had to lock myself in my bedroom, after calling him every name under the sun. Now I didn't give a damn, all my belongings could be broken. I just wanted him back.

I awoke depressed, lonely and terrified on Tuesday 20th, the day Cathal would be buried. Our neighbours came to support us, trying in vain to divert us, getting the breakfast ready. Mary's sister Breda was ill, and my daughter Breda was trying to help her before we set off to the Cathedral for the funeral Mass. For Frances, that morning was 'as surreal as the mornings before':

> My disbelief had abated none. I dressed in something black. No make-up again. Very little food. I was cried out from the day before and numb. I felt like I was walking underwater. Every movement felt laboured. I told Breda that I wished I had a photo of Cathal in the coffin looking dead; I needed that to remember he was gone.

As we entered the Cathedral yard once more we experienced the sympathy of a huge crowd, many of whom had taken time off work to come and pray with us. As I entered this beautiful building, I again saw the grey uniforms of all the students of Thurles Christian Brothers School, who had been marshalled by their principal, An Bráthair Seán Ó Dúgáin. I found this profoundly moving; the most moving part of the funeral rite. I am eternally grateful to An Bráthair Ó Dúgáin for his kindness and support during that time, and for bringing all the students to the funeral. It still moves me when I think of it, because I associate it so closely with Cathal in his school uniform in the coffin before the altar.

One of my past pupils, Gerard O'Brien, a wonderful singer, and now a solicitor working in Thurles, rushed from Dublin to prepare the students for the singing at the funeral Mass. I am still moved to tears when I hear the hymn *Be Not Afraid*. It always reminds me of the sadness of losing Cathal.

> Be not afraid,
> I go before you always,
> Come follow me,
> And I will give you rest.

You shall cross the barren desert,
But you shall not die of thirst.
You shall wander far in safety,
Though you do not know the way.
You shall speak your words in foreign lands,
And all will understand.
You shall see the face of God and live.

With heightened senses every word entered my being. I felt
so lonely listening to its cadences. I pictured the barrenness
and the vastness of the desert; I felt the loneliness of this vast
world stretching far away into the horizon. But, in the midst
of all the horror I found it somehow very healing. It is one of
the most healing memories for me. It made sense of the
funeral rite, not just as a religious one, but as a healing one.
And it has lasted down to this time. I don't go to many
funerals, and when I hear this hymn it brings me back to
February 1990, and I feel the sadness again, for the bereaved,
but mainly for myself.

On that morning surrounded by this vast congregation, I
felt utterly alone. As the priest recited the prayers of the Mass,
which I had heard so often, I stared at the coffin. I imagined
Cathal lying silently in the darkness of the coffin. I wanted to
taste the bitterness of loss. But how I would love to see the
face of my child again. To hear his voice. To see his
mischievous smile. To hear him play the flute, as he teased me
that he was a faster learner than I was. It would never be. I
would never see his face again, nor hear his voice. I felt a
strong desire to open the coffin and look on him; a kind of
despairing thought.

There was another coffin beside his. Another family in
grief. I felt a sense of anger that Cathal did not have this
ceremony for himself. I was also conscious of my family
beside me. I wished I could help them. Make this nightmare

go away. They were engrossed in their own thoughts. Surviving in their own individual ways. Deirdre had strong physical symptoms of distress throughout the Mass, and wrote that she could not control the shaking in her legs. Mentally she was still in shock and cannot recall anything about the Mass or what went on.

Bill recalls trying to be strong. That is how I remember him. I did not see him as a teenager any longer. Mentally I was somehow placing too much of a burden on him. Perhaps he sensed what I was thinking. He felt overawed by the great congregation, and, like Deirdre, does not have many memories of that day:

> I think I was trying to be too strong. I remember wondering how my family would survive this – especially Mam. I did not think she would be able to get through this. I honestly thought she would end up in Clonmel [the psychiatric hospital]. I was thinking more about everyone else than myself.

Breda was angry as well as shocked. It was inconceivable to her that her brother was in a coffin before the altar. This was not fair:

> The church was crowded. Two funerals – he couldn't even have one for himself. I hated being there. I thought I would pass out, I felt so weak. The Mass was a blur; my Uncle Joe & I clung together for support.

I wanted the Mass to go on. The longer it lasted the longer I would be near my child. I did not want it to end at all. But it drew to a close with the words, 'The Mass is ended. Go in peace'. But peace was something I did not know for a long time. The funeral rite that followed remains clear in my

mind. I was drawn into it, experienced every word of a rite
that I had heard so often, but was never moved by it. But now
it had special significance. Every word meant something to
my sensitised mind. One of the prayers in particular rang out
with an unnatural clarity, and seemed to transport me with
the soul of my child being led to Heaven by the angels:

> May the angels lead you into paradise;
> May the martyrs come to welcome you
> And take you to the holy city,
> The new and eternal Jerusalem.
>
> May the choirs of angels welcome you
> And lead you to the bosom of Abraham;
> And where Lazarus is poor no longer
> May you find eternal rest.

My reverie was soon shattered by preparations for the removal
to St Patrick's graveyard. Walking down the aisle after the
coffin was harrowing. I was afraid I would collapse. I wept
uncontrollably, all my anguish pouring out as I walked the
final steps of the journey that had started on Sunday 18th on
the road to the hospital. The beginning of the journey was
one of optimism and hope that my child was not badly
injured; the end was the stumbling footsteps of a grieving
family to the graveyard. Breda recorded what it was like for
her:

> After Mass all his little friends were coming up to us; it
> was heartbreaking, it hurt so much. I'm sure my family
> felt it badly. I was deep in shock & completely
> withdrawn as we walked out behind the hearse. I wanted
> to walk to the graveyard & my uncle Joe came too - a
> miserable twosome, but I couldn't have survived

without Joe. My mother's family are unique. We finally reached the grave & I just stood swaying, feeling as weak as a straw, staring into the hole that was his burial ground, his bed forever. They were lowering down the coffin slowly. I felt dead inside, like I was in a terrible trance.

Frances remembers little about the funeral except,

Cathal's little friend, Patrick, being the last person at the graveside, looking so sad and so lost. I loved him for that and I wish I could tell him that now. He obviously loved my brother, who was probably his partner in crime.

As they lowered the coffin into the earth I put my arms around my family. I wanted to protect them from the brutality of death, to assuage their pain. But nothing could ease that pain, as the dark earth claimed their young brother. We stared at the grave for a while, but were distracted as more people came to sympathise with us. And finally all those who had come to be with us, and share our pain, left the graveyard, and we stood alone, our small family and our close relatives.

The funeral ritual in Ireland has evolved over many centuries. It is normally brought to an end by the family and the community gathering together after the burial for a meal. For some people there may be something healing about gathering in the local village hall, and feeling the warmth of the local community. It is not always possible to do this in large towns like Thurles, and so we made our way to one of the local hotels. I don't have a clear memory of this, but Breda recorded it in her diary shortly afterwards, and, unlike myself, who felt some comfort from being with the extended family, she shows mixed feelings about her experience:

We went back to the Munster Hotel so that our relations & friends could get something to eat. They were everywhere, people putting their arms around me, telling me it was going to be alright, & I hated them for it. How could it be alright? Nothing would ever be right again. I was feeling very angry & very violent. My dad sat for a while with his arms around Fran & me, but I couldn't sit still. I had to find my Uncle Tom. I did find him at the bar & I snuggled into him for some comfort. I knew my dearest uncle was trying to be strong for me. He always is but he was breaking down at times. Despite & because of my loss my love for him at that time felt overpoweringly strong. In the months previous to that we had grown close to each other & I loved him dearly. That day he gave me everything he had & for that I will never forget him.

CHAPTER SIX

Struggling to Cope

*A Prolonged Nightmare of Pessimism, Depression and
Loneliness in a Grief-Stricken Internal World*

AS THE FUNERAL ritual ended, and we returned to
our house, downhearted and sorrowful, the long
road of coping with our loss and reaching some kind
of acceptance began. This first year is an immensely
important period in rehabilitation, and in my ignorance of
bereavement and grieving, I made many fundamental
mistakes, which caused hurt to my children and hindered
rather than promoted their healing. Experiencing the death
of my child has made me an 'expert' on the feelings that are
associated with grief, but how I coped was harsh and lacking
in self-care, both for myself and for some members of my
family. It was in keeping with my personality of the time.

For the moment, however, we had to begin our journey of
recovery as best we could. Our neighbours were at hand for
the first few days. They had been immensely helpful, bringing
food, making sure that those who came were fed, and
generally keeping us company. I had the idea of leaving
Thurles and buying a house elsewhere, but the goodness of
our neighbours made me reconsider, and we have remained
in the same house that we built in 1972.

But life had to go on and we had to set out on our road of
grief as individuals and as a family. Our house became a place
where sorrow was audible in that first week after the funeral.

I often listened and shuddered as I heard the wailing and weeping of various members of my family from different rooms. I felt helpless, and when I was not working I just sat and brooded. The world seemed a dark place. I could see no light, and felt utterly pessimistic. Lethargic. Depressed. Defeated.

Frances has the clearest account of what the first week was like for her:

> Awful apprehension made me full, and I ate very little the whole week I was home. I remember being able to eat only tiny pieces of brown bread with a little cheese. I didn't even care about putting on make-up – which I was rarely seen without. I remember feeling the power Cathal had over me, a power I didn't realise. Breda & I joked about our disinterest in the facade of make-up because Cathal always teased us about how ugly we were without it. Life was reduced to bare bones. Eating tiny bites, no adornments like make-up or jewellery, and deep sleeps at night that I rarely experienced before or after. It was the sleep of the profoundly traumatised – dead and dreamless.

Like her mother, Frances felt that

> Cathal would round the corner on his bike, full of life and laughing at the distress only his presence could lift. I could not, could not believe it. After the funeral I just wanted to get back to America and to leave the despair. I had to borrow the money to return.

Cards of sympathy began to arrive, and at times I felt angry and irritated at this further reminder of our loss. I was not amenable to comfort. The cards seemed to come for a long time, and eventually I wished that they would cease. I have a large box of them in our attic, and as I looked through them when writing this book, I found them very consoling. At the time of our deepest mourning I was too distraught to appreciate them.

Bill recalled his feelings and his thoughts about those first few weeks:

> The funeral passed by in a blur. Family and friends came from afar. A week passed. Family and friends returned to their normal lives. We were on our own now. No longer a full family. Yes, on our OWN. I couldn't face the reality. I tried to pretend my brother's death was a lie, and that I would soon wake up from this awful nightmare. I imagined how Cathal would reappear at any moment. I imagined how I would take hold of him and take him away where I could protect him for the rest of this life. I cared about nothing else. But, as the weeks went on Cathal did not reappear. No matter how much I wished or dreamt, I could not change the situation. I felt an overwhelming sense of loss. No one could possibly imagine how I missed him. I would have given my life for his. I felt helpless knowing how much my family was suffering.
>
> Our home was now a mere shell, barely holding itself together. It was as though there was no future. How could God let such a thing happen? How could there be a future? Is there a God? Where has Cathal gone? Where could I turn to now? ... I envied intact families, now that we were six instead of seven. I didn't want to be the youngest and the only son. I couldn't sleep in the dark as it was too much like death. Part of me wanted to die so that I could be with Cathal again, to take care of him. We were always a good family. My father worked hard. My mother did everything for us. In short we never did

WHEN A CHILD DIES

anything to hurt anybody or anything. Why us? Why not another family? Why was our Cathal taken away from us?

The journals of Mary and myself begin shortly after the first week of Cathal's death, and remind me of how we were. Writing a journal was a suggestion that I made to my family as a way of helping us. I feel that they are a creative and useful aid in the grieving process. I am reminded that I made the decision to return to work, on Friday, 23 February, a mere five days after the most traumatic event in my life. I was tormented sitting around, but my main reason for going back so soon was to get Bill back into study. My motive was good, but this was not the way to go. Bereaved children need time and emotional support, and I did not offer Bill these. I was also aware of my duty to my students, who would be sitting their honours English and Irish Leaving Certificate in a few months.

Their oral Irish examination was also due in a matter of weeks. I worried about how Bill would cope with that. Had I been in my right mind I would have suggested to him that he spend another year in school, and allow him time to grieve. My emphasis was on education rather than care for my remaining son. This, I think, had serious consequences for him in terms of coping with his bereavement. Worse still, I did not stop him from doing his mock Leaving Certificate tests, which were totally irrelevant under the circumstances. He was unable to write very much.

I was still in my inner world of grief when I made my way to school on Friday. I did not think that I would be able to work for the full day, so I decided that Bill and I would go in for the last two classes. Looking back I realise that I was beginning to operate again, perhaps in a male way of keeping busy. My journal shows how I was thinking at that time:

I opened the staffroom door with a sense of apprehension, and was greatly relieved when I found it empty. The experience of conducting two classes that evening was dreadful, but at least I had proven that I could do so, and it was a small step on the road to rehabilitation for me, and especially for Bill. I did not delay that evening, and did not meet any of the teachers, for which I was grateful.

Yet it was an unreal experience. I noted the grim faces of my fifth year students, and I could hear my voice as if it was detached from me.

I lived in my own grief-stricken world. The outside world was an alien place. I did not want to live in this alien place. I wanted to die. I prayed many times for this to happen, to be near my child. I thought of all the good things that I had in my life, especially the comfort of my house, and said to myself that I would willingly swap this and live in a tent on the roadside, if only I had my son back. Going into the supermarket at the end of the first week was traumatic. I felt blinded by the bright lights, and conscious of people looking at me. This bright world was not my world, and I wanted to escape home as quickly as possible.

Not long after Cathal's funeral, the parents of the driver came to see us. It took a lot of courage for them to come. They looked downcast and sad. But, what was there to say? I recall my feelings as a combination of lethargy, anger, indifference and embarrassment. I was too exhausted to offer them any consolation. But I don't suppose I would have done so one way or the other, because my primary feeling was one of anger at their daughter.

One person who came to the house talked at length about how awful it was for the driver to have killed someone. I was filled with rage at this, but remained silent. I have heard others say that it is worse to kill somebody than to be killed. It is surely an awful thing to be responsible for the death of another. I have no doubt that it evokes much long-term pain and guilt, but I doubt very much if it can equal the pain of the family of the dead child. There are no winners in this situation.

I was also angered by rumours that were spread, a phenomenon that is often associated with death in Ireland. Some people spread the rumour that Cathal's sister had been home from America and brought him the bike on which he was killed. Others said that he had been wearing earphones and did not hear the car coming. People do not mean to be malicious, but such rumours add to the pain of the bereaved, especially as in Cathal's case they were untrue. The truth was that Cathal had been careless, and he did not hear the car because another car was coming behind him and it blotted out the noise. (The driver of this car, who witnessed the accident, was Mark's father. Mark became Breda's husband.)

I was also enraged when a letter arrived addressed to Cathal. I opened it and discovered it was a bill from the hospital for the ambulance. I wrote an angry letter to the person who sent the bill. Now I am sorry that I did so. It must have greatly hurt that individual. Nevertheless, I hope that such institutions are more sensitive nowadays.

My diary entry for the end of that first week reveals a disturbed and tormented mind:

> The first weekend following Cathal's death was one of unrelieved misery and depression for me, despite the fact that Margaret [Mary's sister] was there to keep us company. Sunday was simply a nightmare. At 11 o'clock Mass in the Cathedral I felt that many eyes were fixed upon us. I hoped some were praying for us. I felt Mary's distress beside me, and dreaded the moment when the

priest would read out the list of dead. I had sometimes imagined my own name being read out, but never this. It was a total nightmare to hear the words 'prayers are requested for the happy repose of the soul of Cathal O'Shea, The Furze'. I tried to suppress my emotion as the unreal words re-echoed in my mind.

After dinner I sat by the fire looking at my watch, and counting the minutes to the time that the accident had occurred. At 3 o'clock I said to myself that at that time last Sunday Cathal had only two hours to live, that he had been at the bridge chatting to his friend P.J., and was enjoying the sunshine, oblivious to the fact that within an hour he would be lying unconscious on the road, the victim of a cruel accident, and that within another hour he would be with God. It was totally unbelievable. I followed the hands of the clock as they remorselessly moved on. There was no way of putting that clock back. My eyes remained on it until four and the tension eased a little when the hands moved beyond that hour.

I continued with that behaviour for several weeks. I felt desperately lonely, and was almost overwhelmed with the sense of loss. I felt a need to somehow reach out to the public, and I wrote a letter to the local paper, the *Tipperary Star*, in the second week after Cathal's death. One paragraph shows some of the feelings and thoughts I had at that time:

> Our pain at the moment is impossible to describe and only those who have endured a similar loss could understand it. We in turn now understand what other people have suffered and only now can we share in this suffering. Cathal's death has changed our lives, and changed it for the better. We can never be the same

again; we can never feel bitterness or envy or any thoughts that would sully our child's name, because Cathal's greatest and most noticeable trait was his complete sense of forgiveness. We loved him for his good nature and his liveliness, which filled our house with laughter for the last decade. We know his spirit will always be in our house and when our turn comes to die we know he will come to help us. We no longer fear death. We now have someone to care for us.

As I re-read the letter now I am amazed at how logical and well-constructed it is despite the pain I was in at the time. I suppose the lesson is that we never know how people are feeling by their outward behaviour.

Like me, Bill was trying to pull himself together, but was equally disorientated and distracted,

> ... devastated. Angry. Sad. Why? Broken. Confused. Not reality. Unsure. How could we go on? Deeply missed him. How could I go back to school? Felt I had to be strong. Going back to school was big for me. I remember trying to be strong for my Dad as we both went back to school together.

While I have berated myself about how I cared for my surviving teenage son, I think that going back to school was helpful insofar as Bill was surrounded by his friends. He had many good friends, and they still occasionally meet. He also lived at home, although it was a sad and sorrowful place. Breda and Frances had to return to foreign countries, and cope as best they could. Deirdre worked in Dublin and could come home at the end of the week. She writes about the dread she felt at seeing us at weekends:

The sadness in our home was overwhelming, and I felt
so utterly helpless to do anything to ease the pain and
heartache. I was afraid to pass Cathal's bedroom door
for such a long time. I used to shiver with fear passing
the closed door at night. I dreaded getting up during the
night, and passing the door. I felt great anger at that girl
for crashing into Cathal.

Breda had depended upon her Uncle Tom for support, but
he, too, had to return to London to work, and she clutched
at whatever support she could get:

> Throughout the next few days my good friends were
> around me. Steve [a Pallottine brother], whom I'd
> known for years, came down from Dublin & spent ages
> trying to break through my icy exterior & get me to cry.
> He said I was like a stone, impassive. But the pain in my
> eyes was unbearable. He didn't succeed, but I loved him
> for trying. My ex-boyfriend was down a lot, but then he's
> like part of our family. We used to take Cathal out with
> us. He didn't know what to say to me, but he held me
> for hours one night, & just having somebody's arms
> around me was enough. I couldn't cry, but I needed
> some security. Then a friend came over. I felt he could
> help me ... We talked for hours about Cathal & I told
> him how I felt, & he held me & took away some of my
> pain. He made me feel something, some emotion, & I
> needed that. But I still couldn't cry.
>   Gradually my relations drifted home, a bunch of
> extraordinary people. Fran & I had to go back to work.
> I couldn't face it. Tom was coming to Dublin & I would
> go back with him. So, two weeks after the death of
> Cathal I packed my bags & my family dropped me into
> the station for a lonely train trip to Dublin. At that

point the ice broke & I cracked up – my heart was torn apart. I didn't want to go. I clung to my family, each of us in tears. I stood by the door all the way up, crying & smoking & fighting to stay sane. Tom and Breda met me & Tom went to Gran & Granddad's. I think he couldn't cope with my pain at all ...

Breda spent that night in Dublin. It was a 'restless night' for her and the following day she set out on her 'lonely trip' to London, accompanied by her uncle Tom, who talked to her and tried to help her. She recorded how helpless and defeated she felt as Tom and his wife Vourneen tried to protect her when she reched their house in London:

Inside I didn't think I would make it this time. The fighter in me was dead. Or so it seemed. The next day reality hit home, & when I sat at the table surrounded by Tom, Vourneen & their complete and intact little family of three boys, I just went crazy & started crying & ran out of the room. Tom took me to my bedroom & lay on the bed with me & cried with me for a long time. I can't explain how I felt really. It must be like knowing the world will end within five minutes. Total desolation. I was falling apart. Tom took me back to my flat later & the lonely ache droned away inside me. I hadn't eaten in days at that stage. I felt I never would again. I was alone now. I had my flatmate. She was great, but she had her own worries. My family was in Ireland & Tom had enough on his plate. I was miserably alone, so I decided I must build up a wall of resistance for myself. I had to survive.

It was a case of survival for all of us. I was really anxious about how Mary would cope. I feared for her mental safety, and this prompted me at times to put on a brave face. But this was not always possible. How can a father conceal the anguish he feels when his child has been killed? I now realise that being vulnerable, and being seen to be so, would have been more appropriate. Mary always allowed herself to be vulnerable, and vulnerability is a real sign of strength. It allows us to reach out; it gives out the message to others that it is ok to show feelings. Mary wrote about how she allowed her tears to flow as she met people in Thurles:

> One of the hardest steps I took was to go to the post office to cancel the children's allowance. I remember saying to the assistant, 'what do you do about children's allowance when a child dies', and then I broke down in front of him. I have cried several times talking to people in the shops, but didn't feel embarrassed. Crying seems to be my only outlet.

There is nothing as tender and as precious as a mother's love for her child. I have always been very sad when I see this reflected in her account:

> I missed not having washing & ironing to do for Cathal, and generally taking care of him. He loved his big bowls of cornflakes or Weetabix, and I miss not having to buy these anymore ... I didn't bake for a long time after Cathal died, as I would be thinking he'd love whatever it was I was making. I still find myself thinking of him a lot when I cook something he liked.

So great was her disbelief that for the next year she expected him to arrive home from school at 4.15 p.m. She had given up her career to look after her children, and they always arrived home from school to find their dinner on the table.

I was amazed at how Mary seemed to cope in the midst of her pain. This pain was best reflected in one particular section of her journal:

> Something I forgot to mention was that I couldn't open the window in Cathal's room for ages, as his special smell was all over the room, and I wanted it like that. In fact, now that the window is open I feel that smell is still there. The other thing was that I wanted to hurt myself physically – like run through briars – because I believed that Cathal must have suffered some pain, even though they said that he couldn't have felt anything.

I found this so utterly sad; and Frances records how heart-rending this was for her:

> One of our most poignant conversations was when Mam told me that she kept Cathal's room as airtight as possible to keep his smell in. She would sit in there and smell him. One day, several months later, my Dad innocently opened the windows. When mam went in she was hysterical. I relived that scene over and over, crying desperately for my mother. Oh the profound wound to the soul of a mother who gave everything for her children!

Yet, despite her crushing pain Mary found the strength to go to the post office to cancel the children's allowance. But she showed even greater strength when it came to moving on a little and restoring his room. For me this step shows that we were beginning to regain some control, although at the time it didn't feel like that, and there was no question of giving away all of his stuff. His belongings were precious to us. Mary and I discussed this at length, and decided we would give away his good clothes. It was an extremely hard decision, but somehow it gave us a little more strength to travel the road of grief. Mary probably understates our sadness when we did this:

> I gave his good clothes to a little friend of his a few weeks after his death. This wasn't easy, and when his mother was gone with them I cried for a long time. We also tried to get his room back to normal, bit by bit. I still have just a few little things belonging to him. It was heartbreaking to go into his room for the first few weeks.

We kept some of his stuff, including many stories and poems that he wrote, a few items of clothing, his copies and school books, a small electronic game, a few letters and cards that he created, and his caul. We gave some items to our surviving children. When I had completed this book I gave the remainder of his stuff to my children. These were copies, drawings, Ladybird books, a few letters, and cards which had been stored in the attic for the last eighteen years. We still have his caul and an album of photographs of him at various times in his short life.

—◦━✦━◦—

CHAPTER SEVEN

Will This Pain Ever End?

Anniversaries are Approached with Dread,
and their Passing Greeted with Relief

MY FEELINGS OF intense fear and terror continued unabated for several months. The sense of loss was almost overwhelming. Waking up in the morning was the hardest. I was blinded by what seemed like a great light draining the energy from me and every morning this huge light held me fast in its glare. The words 'Cathal is dead' stood out in deep black across that bright light. Mary, too, woke up to the same torment:

> I find the morning time the hardest. I think of him the minute I wake up. I live one day at a time now. It's the loneliness that's so very hard to cope with. I find that I panic a bit when I realise that I won't see Cathal today or tomorrow.

In those early weeks and months we all struggled to do our daily tasks. Nothing seemed worthwhile anymore. My doctor put me on anti-depressant tablets to help me cope, but as far as I could see they did nothing to lessen the pain. My spirituality helped me, but other members of the family did not have the same experience. My colleagues in Thurles CBS often told me that I was strong and would come to terms with my loss. I did not want to hear this. I did not feel strong. I felt that I was barely managing. I know that they had sympathy for me, but what could they do? What could they say? It's so difficult to say the 'right thing'. I suppose some people have not experienced bereavement personally, or may not have resolved their own grief, and find it difficult to know what to say. Sometimes they look for a formula, but silence and merely being with the bereaved is often the best comfort. I'm glad that they didn't offer me religious consolation and well-meant platitudes. I hated it when people said, 'he's an angel in Heaven'. I didn't want him in Heaven. I wanted him with me on earth.

My sadness was increased because the wife of one of my colleagues had died around this time. The entries in my journal for that first week back at school show how difficult teaching was for me. I noted my behaviour in the Leaving Certificate English and Irish classes for one of those days:

> I was very conscious of Bill, and could see that mentally he was far away, staring vacantly ahead, oblivious of what I was saying, unable to concentrate. In my ignorance of the process of grief I tried to haul him back, and asked him a question on the text. He burst out crying, and I went down to comfort him. Sharing grief knows no embarrassment, and I was not worried that the class should see us like this. I said to him 'we can do it, Bill, we can do it, and you will be alright'. He stopped crying and said he was sorry, to which I replied that there was no need to apologise.
>
> I went to the lovely little school oratory on my way out of class. I had rarely visited there before, because I had never felt the need to, and when I did I was only conscious of how pleasant it was. Now I knelt in front of the Blessed Sacrament and prayed desperately to Jesus to help me get through the next class at 9.50 a.m.,

which was Honours Irish. Bill was also in that class. I was supposed to be doing conversation with them, but felt unable to recall the difficult vocabulary, which is necessary at that level, so I allowed them to practise among themselves.

Going into the oratory between each class became the norm for me over the next few months. I realise now just how insensitive I had been in the previous years in dealing with bereaved students. Without thinking I assumed that they could just come back to school and continue as if nothing had happened. School can be a cruel place at times. Eighteen years later and teachers are much more sensitive to their students' needs. As a principal I was forever complaining about lack of resources, but they are far better today than in 1990. It is, however, the awareness of teachers that really counts. In that context, loss has made me acutely aware of how young people feel when confronted with loss and grieving. When I now read of my children's distress I realise that extreme sensitivity and empathy is necessary in school.

Life at work was equally difficult for our three daughters. Deirdre, I feel, understates how hard it was for her, and certainly did not realise how painful it was for me. I think I wanted to spare my family the added pain of seeing how devastated I was, and often concealed my pain. That is how I thought then, and how I coped came from that belief. Now I think differently. I feel that parents should allow their children to see their sorrow, and to hear them express it. This gives their children permission to show their own grief. Deirdre states this very well as she reveals her own loneliness and worries:

The first few weeks were extremely traumatic. I didn't want to return to Dublin to work. I wanted to stay at home. I remember my employer giving me two weeks off work, but I didn't want to leave Mam on her own all day. I couldn't understand how my dad returned to work so soon after Cathal's death, how he was able to go back to the school – he seemed so detached to me. He was very much a closed book, and it seemed impossible to penetrate what appeared to be a hard exterior to reveal his innermost feelings. It was in much later years that I learned of the brutal effect Cathal's death had on my father. My mother, on the other hand, expressed her grief openly, thus allowing us to grieve and receive a certain level of comfort and solace. But, I worried about Mam so much and how she would recover, or ever feel any sense of happiness again.

Like Deirdre, Breda quickly passes over coping with work; it is easy to see the feelings of depression and emptiness in her life, as well as some relief at being occupied again:

Going to work the next day was very hard. I had no interest in work now; the thrill of it was gone completely. They were very good to me: a potted plant sat on my desk & a card & my friends came up in ones telling me they were glad I was back. In a way so was I; as lonely as I was, I felt I would never go home again. I couldn't live there without Cathal.

Apart from one person, Frances did not experience the same degree of care or friendship from her co-workers as Breda did:

My first day back at work, another Irish girl, Sheila, just burst out crying when she saw me. She had sent a beautiful flower arrangement for the funeral. This was significant because we were not friends. But her sincere sorrow forged a bond then that grew into a close friendship.

The people at Pete's [Tavern] sent nothing, not even a card. The occasion went unacknowledged. It was then I first understood the fragility of human relationships, and the rarity of real love. I was not embittered but I felt completely & utterly alone.

What kept Frances going in the midst of her almost insane mindset in a workplace devoid of compassion was the memory of how her mother had allowed her the space to grieve, and how they allowed their vulnerability to show:

From the first, Mammy insisted that we talk about Cathal, although she and we broke down at the mention of his name. This was not an attempt at pop psychology – a mother exhorting her children to vent their pain and grief. This was Cathal's mother, his fierce protector in death as in life. Determined to keep him alive no matter the cost in tears and searing pain. Determined to give him life again ... with her memories, with her words married to our words. Determined that he would always be with us, part of us. She never censored her feeling with us, and I cherished that. I believe that a special closeness forms when peoples share pain.

As I struggled to cope with work, my own grief, and the pain of watching how my family suffered, I lived from hour to hour. I found it hard to contemplate a day, not to mention a week or a month, passing since Cathal died. It was beyond me to think in terms of a year. I could never imagine eighteen years passing. For the first few months I was always uneasy. I had no peace of mind, no peace in my heart. I often waited for someone to call; just to have the company of someone who was not going through the pain of grief. I often prayed that someone would come, and waited expectantly. But it never happened. It was so lonely. So empty.

One Sunday, about two weeks after Cathal died, I was so uneasy that I could not sit, stand, lie or walk. I did not feel suicidal, but I felt that I could not make it through the day. I felt that I was going insane. In the midst of this helplessness I thought of Fr James Meehan, the parish priest of New Inn, which is a parish adjacent to Cashel. He had once been a curate in Thurles, and was a saintly person. As a schoolboy, I often went to confession to him to confess my 'impure thoughts and desires,' which were the bane of teenagers' lives in the early sixties, and brought beads of perspiration to the brows of many a young person in the confessional! He was always so gentle, and used the term 'dear soul' when addressing the fearful young penitent.

Somehow I felt that Fr Meehan could bring some ease to me, and help me make it through that Sunday. Mary and Deirdre agreed to come with me. We were welcomed with his usual kindness. I remember he put his hands over us and prayed for a considerable length of time in Latin. My school Latin had long been forgotten, but this sounded so powerful. I did not feel alone. I sensed a greater power. I felt some strength returning, and that disabling sensation of unease abating. I remember driving home and thinking that I would be able to get through that Sunday, and that next day I would be back in the routine of work. It was a question of crawling slowly along that road of early grieving. Mary does not really remember going to Fr Meehan, and said that it doesn't seem to have made any impression on her or helped her.

Bill, too, was seized with fear, anxiety and despair. He experienced some of the thoughts and emotions that I had in the early days. He wrote that he was fearful of what the future holds. Things will never be the same again, and I knew it ... I felt tired but couldn't sleep. My brain was working overtime with thoughts and impulses ... I longed for a decent night's sleep, but I did not get it. I broke into cold sweats as unimaginable thoughts crucified me. I felt hollow, and the mere sight of food made me sick. I looked to other people for help – regular visits to the church, the doctor, good friends, until I painfully realised that no one could help me. Best friend, old friend, new friend, not even my girlfriend could help me. This was the moment when the feeling of utter despair set upon me. I was left with a vacuum inside me. A huge hole that could be filled by nothing.

What was I to do? Was there anything I could do? Was there any way out apart from actually taking my own life? If I had the courage I think I would have done so. The pain was incomprehensible, and there seemed to be no cure. I spent hours at the graveside staring at the clay. I wanted to be with him. Why should I be deprived in such a way? I tried to conjure up images, memories, but to no avail. I was mixed up. I could not think straight. I found it difficult to remember. How could I be so cruel? How could I not remember my own brother properly?

Time moved on, and dragged us with it. At that time I visited the grave each day on my way home from school. With some type of macabre instinct I pictured my child deep in the grave in his school uniform. I pictured him and his uniform rotting. That is the reality of death, who had pushed his brutal face close to mine. I stood, always in disbelief, looking at the brown clay, neatly heaped and awaiting its headstone, and wondered if the pain would ever cease.

The first public reminder we had of Cathal's death was the month's mind. I found it hard to believe that a full month had passed. The intensity of the pain of loss had not subsided. I made arrangements for the month's mind with my disbelief as strong as ever. I listened to the priest's introductory words, 'this Mass is the month's mind Mass for the repose of the soul of Cathal O'Shea, The Furze', with dread. I was aware of being in the public view again and felt self-conscious and ill at ease. I could hear Mary silently sobbing beside us. It was an ordeal for me. But it was the first milestone on my journey of grief, the first anniversary of several more to come within the next twelve months. At each one I always tried to see how far I had advanced on the road to recovery. They were like signposts of progress. Going to the grave after that Mass had a special significance. One month dead. Still desolate. Four families on this back road had lost children before Cathal was killed. The only two boys in one of these families had died; one of them was killed just above our house. I felt that they would understand how I was feeling. I asked some of them how long this pain would last. They looked pessimistic, and never really answered me. When I talked recently to Mary about the intensity of the pain in 1990 and my wish that it would ease, she said that she did not have such thoughts. She simply suffered on in silence.

I began to experience somatic symptoms from the stress of my bereavement. The skin peeled off my hands, and one evening at tea I felt a tightening of my chest. I was convinced that I was going to have a heart attack. I could feel my breath shortening. I went to my doctor, who was profoundly sympathetic, and who had visited us on one occasion to comfort us and felt some relief when she explained that this had nothing to do with my heart, but was simply a tightening of the muscles due to stress.

My memory was badly affected. I had to make lists to remind me of what I needed to do. There were many times when I was making my way to Thurles, which is only two miles away, that I had to stop the car and try to remember where I was going, and why I was going there. It was dangerous for me to drive in that first month. I had never realised that grief could affect anyone like this. On several occasions I had some near misses on the road. I remember one evening coming home from my uncle's house, and unthinkingly crossed the main road as a car was coming towards me.

I had also forgotten that I had applied to examine the oral Irish for the Leaving Certificate, which was held about a month after Cathal's death. I was shocked when I got the letter of appointment from the Department, and I worried about Bill doing the examination so soon after the death of his brother. I wrote a note to the examiner explaining what had happened, and asking that he should not ask Bill questions about his family. I realise now that I should never have allowed Bill to sit that examination, nor should I have proceeded to examine students myself. I should have contacted the Department of Education, and asked to be excused. It was not altogether professional to embark upon examining students in my frame of mind. The school designated to me was the Christian Brothers School, Portlaoise. I mentioned to the principal that my son had been killed the previous month. As principal, he was rightly more concerned about the welfare of his pupils than about my plight, and as I was examining one of the students he arrived in the room and sat and listened, as he was entitled to do. I understood, but I was enraged that he should have thought that I was unable to do my job! He seemed to be satisfied, and despite my pain I successfully examined over one hundred students.

Around this time I felt that it would be appropriate to put together an album of photographs of Cathal. I gathered over seventy photographs, and found it unbearable to look at them. They brought my child to life again, but only on paper. The first photograph shows him as a baby in his little white seat. He has a lovely smile in that photograph and it broke my heart to look at it. Beside that is a photo of our baby up on the table with Bill, sitting on a pile of my Ph.D. notes. Mary typed my Ph.D. dissertation on an old manual typewriter, and she used to put Cathal sitting in his white chair on the table so that she could mind him. The album shows Cathal dressed in his many funny outfits, wearing masks, playing a guitar (tennis racket), dressed in his cowboy boots, making funny faces, getting his First Communion, getting Confirmation, and showing off his new suit. I have only looked at this album a few times, and each time it is difficult for me to endure it. We put up some photographs of Cathal around the house, and I often found myself staring at them, and still disbelieving that this is all I had left of my child.

I am an avid reader, but in that first month I was unable to read. I have never read fiction since. I always loved fiction before our tragedy, but the reality of death was so brutal and so absolute that I find it difficult to enjoy fiction to this day. Reality is what matters to me. But, I began looking at television within the first few months. For me, the television was company. It was like a friend. Most importantly it did not require effort. I was so exhausted from the expending of nervous energy and stress, and the effort to do my work, that it was a relief just to sit and watch. As well as that I found myself absorbed in whatever programme I was watching, and this gave me relief from the pain.

One of the saddest memories I have was the death of our cocker spaniel, Dotty, shortly after Cathal died. The sadness stems from the connection with Cathal. Both were the same age. I remember bringing her home when Cathal was an infant. We had a small red mini-van at the time, and all our children were in the back cuddling their new black pup, and minding their new baby brother. Little did we think that our dog would outlive our new child.

Dotty's heart was failing, and we took her to the vet hoping that something might be done. The vet, however, advised that she be put asleep. Bill was only four when we got Dotty, and, like the rest of the family, has a great love of animals. He came to town with us that evening, but did not come to the vet. Unfortunately, we met him on our way home coming out of Rossa Street, a small narrow street on which Thurles Christian Brothers School is located. We stopped, and he came to the car and looked in the window. He saw that Dotty was not with us, and guessed that she had been put down. I felt heartbroken at the look of sadness on his face as he turned and walked away.

There was no discernable escape from our sadness during the first year. We made every effort to cope as best we could and began to go out more in an effort to distract ourselves from our pain. One Sunday we decided to go to the Glen of Aherlow with its beautiful scenery. We sat on the wall overlooking the valley, and gazed at the lovely Galtee Mountains towering over the patchwork of green fields. But, our hearts were heavy. Even this small element of enjoyment eluded us. I felt a dull ache in my heart as I drove to the Aherlow House Hotel. There was a large crowd of children there who had received First Holy Communion. They were dressed in their new clothes, and reminded me of how happy Cathal was on the day he made his First Communion. He had a lovely new suit, and looked so innocent as we took some photographs on the lawn of the presbytery.

I looked longingly at the happy faces of the children and their parents, and sadly at the pain-filled faces of Mary and

Deirdre. I felt I had to get away from this happy scene. I did not envy those fortunate parents, but their merriment and enjoyment only increased my sense of loss.

Still, we did not give up in our effort to find some kind of normality, or to escape momentarily from our grief. One of our neighbours asked us to go to Killarney for a few days. But the lovely scenery there was no more successful in clearing our sorrowful mood than the Glen of Aherlow had been. I felt utterly miserable as I drove through scenery that would normally have lifted my spirits. I just wanted to be at home, where I could be myself, and where I could go to my room and cry. I often went to Cathal's room to vent my sorrow alone. This was once Frances's room, and when she left home there were times when I went there and wept at losing her to America. But this was different. I knew that Frances was alive and would occasionally return. Cathal would never come back. Now we were left with an empty room. It would always be a reminder.

The only relief I really got was how well Mary seemed to be coping, although she does not fully agree that she was coping well. I feel, nevertheless, that she greatly understates her distress in her journal. She noted how she felt three months after his death:

> I have to say that I don't feel as desperate as I used to. It has got a little easier, although it's still painful. I would like to mention here things I did to try and heal myself. I go to town a fair bit. I visit a neighbour a few times a week. I also joined a voluntary organisation, but only when I felt ready to do so. I play badminton a lot.

We had very kind friends on our badminton team. They were a good-humoured lot, and did their best to cheer us up. Badminton requires a lot of concentration, and this momentarily diverted us from our sorrow. We were also aware that one of the women on the badminton team had lost her brother in a cruel accident five years earlier. She lived quite near us and was a member of one of the bereaved families mentioned earlier. We felt that she understood.

The year 1990 passed and it was such a relief when it finally came to an end. I always had a habit on New Year's Eve of jokingly saying to Mary that the next year would bring much luck and prosperity. It was a feel-good thought. I had said the same on New Year's Eve, 1989. This is a habit that I no longer indulge. The arrival of spring and summer did not mean much to our family, preoccupied as we were with our grief. I always loved spring, when the birds began their joyful chorus. Having been born in a beautiful upland area of forest, birds and wild creatures meant a lot to me. But following Cathal's death, the summer sunshine went unnoticed, and the cloud of gloom persisted. Winter was better suited to our mood.

Yet, at the end of 1990, while my pain was still severe, my journal indicated some element of relief. This was due, I think, to the anniversaries and special occasions that we had experienced. They had brought us much distress, but enduring them also brought some healing. All of our birthdays were sad occasions because one of our family was not, and would never be, there to celebrate with us. The first anniversary for Cathal was his birthday, which fell on Monday 26 November. He would have been fourteen. It is difficult to describe our pain on that first birthday after his death. The joy that we would have felt was converted to sorrow and a profound feeling of loss. I tried, unsuccessfully, to put this from my mind. What was there to say? What could I do? The old feelings of anger and powerlessness returned with a vengeance. It was such a relief for us when that day ended, and we could, albeit subconsciously, look forward.

Christmas was not far away. We approached it with dread.

As the youngest member of our family, Christmas had held a special excitement for Cathal. He took a certain delight in seeing his daddy prepare the Christmas dinner, and loved helping me put up the Christmas tree. As Christmas Day approached I found myself glancing more and more at the bowl he had brought us the previous year, and my heart was breaking. I had often heard people say that Christmas was a sad time, but could never understand this in the context of how joyful it had always been for us. Now I understood. The empty chair spoke for itself. This was worse than his birthday anniversary. Our little family ate our meal in a sombre and sad mood, and quietly waited for the day to pass. This continued for a number of years, with the pain getting less each year, but always there.

Like Mary and I, Deirdre dreaded those anniversaries:

> Birthdays and anniversaries were all so hard. The pain in the early years was so very strong on those significant days. Sitting in the church and hearing Cathal's name spoken by the priest was extremely painful. Watching Mam break down, constantly looking for her reactions to everything was excruciating. Always thinking about what age he would have been, how he would have performed with the Inter and Leaving Cert. The build-up to those days in the early years was as bad as the actual day. Again, anger and pain and grief were the prime feelings in the early years. Also being unable to get Cathal out of my mind for the first few years. Every day I would have him in my head non-stop.

Frances remarked that anniversaries did not have

the impact they were supposed to. It was little, seemingly unremarkable, unsolicited things that undid me. I could never have prepared for them. They came at inopportune times and in inopportune places. And I just broke down.

Now on Cathal's birthday I think how he would probably be married with children, and be very handsome. I think how it would be to hug the man, Cathal. I think he would have made me feel safe. It still seems so unfair. When my family is all together, his absence is palpable. I think he should be here.

Bill does not dwell on anniversaries. He recalls that they were very sad occasions, 'an opportunity to relive the pain ... very sad watching how it affects others, especially Mam'. He found them easier with the passing of years, 'but still very sad. Learning to live with them. But, Cathal will never be back and there will always be a void in our lives'.

He recalls what the first year was like for him. I feel remorseful at not taking better care of him, and I hope that other parents who read this book will take notice of what he says about these first twelve months, and allow their children time and a safe place to grieve:

Wow! My life completely changed. Cathal died, I did my Leaving Cert., moved to a new life in Dublin and started college. It was a whirlwind. I should not have done this. It was not normal. I was forced to work in London that summer. This was a huge mess for me and a huge mistake. I hated it, and never wanted to be away from home. So much disruption in such a short period of time. STUPID.

Anyway, I moved on. Made new friends. Lived in a dirty, smelly kip of a bedsit on my own ... I always regret not moving in with other people for company. I spent the first year in college coming back to Thurles every

Wednesday night. I did three days a week out of five for most weeks in college as I simply did not want to be in Dublin. I was sad, lonely, confused and living in chaos. But I got through it. I missed Cathal and my life in Thurles.

It was crazy. Somehow, despite my experience that it was neither possible nor desirable to run from grief, I had the idea that going to London would be sufficient to distract us, and bring us some relief from the heaviness that lay upon us. I had been going there to work on building sites since 1985, and it seemed to me that such work would take our minds off our pain. It would also help us financially for Bill's time in college. I made all these decision as if we could pick up life as normal. I had never really thought about what I had done until I read Bill's response to my questionnaire. When I talked to Mary recently I sensed her anger that I had made this decision. Again, I think that it may be a male thing; getting going, getting involved, working to forget, seeking normality through everyday activities, trying to create order out of chaos.

I found work for Bill and myself on the Chelsea and Westminster Hospital building site in Fulham Road. Mary got a job in a hotel. I suppose the only positive thing was that we were near Breda for a few months. But I was very foolish if I imagined that being in London would distract me from my grief. My internal world was grief. I carried that feeling as I trudged around the site carrying heavy loads as a labourer with Gallagher Contractors. When I think of it, we did not have the comfort of home to safely vent our sorrow. We had to bury it to cope with this change.

I was used to building sites in London, but this was the first time that Bill had ever been on one. Large building sites to unseasoned people like ourselves are formidable, and to the uninitiated are stressful. They are not places for sentiment or grief, but where people are driven and sacked at will. We were fortunate in that we knew the foreman, who was more than kind to us. But, by bringing Bill to such an alien place I added to the severe stress of his loss, and I feel that it may have contributed to keeping him stuck in grief. By being stuck, much of his feelings of grief were buried, except rage and envy and disbelief, feelings that can rarely be subdued. These feelings were magnified by seeing our family struggle, and affected his behaviour:

> Time passed. I ceased visiting the grave. People moved on and changed. I was stuck as I watched life slowly passing me by. I was stranded in the trenches of grief. The loneliness was unbearable. I began to resent other families even more and became envious of their happiness. Over and over again I asked the question, 'Why did this have to happen to us?' Hostility set in and I was provoked more easily ... any little thing seemed to upset me. I began to endanger relationships. I began to realise that I was finished with my girlfriend, but had not the will to break the relationship up.
>
> Some people react to death by going into depression or by turning to alcohol or drugs. For me I tried to block the whole affair out. The hardest thing was watching my family suffer, more especially the plight of my parents. My father continued to work hard, but he had grown old. His face was sunken. My mother was much the same. She had dark circles under her eyes. Not a day passed by when she would not cry her eyes out. She could neither eat, drink nor sleep properly any more. She loved her son. She loved all her children, but we knew that she had a special place in her heart for her youngest child. Now everybody worried about her

survival. How could she possibly get over this? She had been the perfect mother and this was the thanks she got for it. How could this happen to such a gentle woman?

Deirdre married Denis within a year of Cathal's death. She loved Denis and found him a great source of consolation and healing. But, like Bill, she worried about her mother, and about leaving home so soon after the trauma:

> I still remember Mam standing at the front door after my honeymoon the night I left to live in Killoran. I was not ready to leave. It was too soon after Cathal. I found it so very hard. I just wanted to be at home, to be there for Mam as she was so alone each day. I still feel great sadness thinking of this. I just needed more time, a few more years at home after what had happened to us as a family.
> When Martin was born on 18 November 1991 I felt immense grief over Cathal. It was not that I didn't love my tiny baby, but with my love came the harsh reality of the extreme grief that my parents had to contend with on the death of their child.

For Frances, that first year was one of devastation, disorientation and despair:

> During the day I looked and acted normally. But at night a monster emerged. I would stay up for hours, hysterically crying, smashing plates, playing music as loudly as possible. My boyfriend was not at all equipped to deal with me. We were a toxic pair, but the fact that he had spent time with my family for two summers when we were intact, the fact that he knew Cathal bound me to him. I simply could not imagine being

with someone who couldn't conceive Cathal and all that he was. He tried to comfort me, but I lashed out at him. He endured me for a year. When I look back, his patience was remarkable. I overdosed, albeit only on aspirin, three times. I wanted to be dead. I was extremely volatile in my relationship with this man, and utterly uncontrollable. One day I was calling home to ask Mammy if Cathal and Bill were ok. I told him that I had a terrible feeling something was wrong with one of them. I had the phone in my hand dialling. He shouted, 'Frances, Cathal is dead. He's dead'. This was months after his death. I went ballistic.

After my third attempt with a bottle of aspirin, this man told me he couldn't take anymore and I had to go home. I knew that was true. I felt I too would be dead if I didn't get help.

Breda, then aged twenty-two, has kept the most detailed account of how she was after a year, and outlined this in her journal of 29 January 1991. It highlights, among other things, sadness, insecurity and awareness of how easily life can be snuffed out. Like her siblings she worried about other members of the family, especially Mary and me:

Almost a year now since Cathal's death. How do I feel? The empty feeling & searing stomach pains are gone. Now I feel bitterness & loneliness when I think of him. After a year you have had time to think & in some ways accept the loss, but there is an added part to your personality that affects you in every walk of life; happiness is a rare feeling now because my thoughts always wander back to that fatal day when our lives were blown apart. I have a terrible feeling of insecurity, a feeling that nothing I have will permanently last, my job, my boyfriend, & my family mostly. The last two naturally will not last forever, but now I fear for the safety of them daily. For example, I love my boyfriend very much. I have poured effort and love into him to recompense somehow for my loss, & he loves me as much, but there's always a fear lurking there that he will leave me, that I will stop loving him, or that some act of God will part us. It frightens me to death, & because I feel this way I'm constantly irritable & uptight, subconsciously trying to push him away even though I want him to stay.

Because of my experience I am doing & saying things I would otherwise never say because I was always the type of person who sat back and enjoyed what I had while it was there. The conclusion I have come to is that in a case like this you really need your family to talk to more than anything; you need to be able to cry & let out all those pent-up emotions that weigh you down. Alternatively you need professional help. I have neither of these, one, because I'm here, & two, because I'm scared to seek that help. As a result I feel a lot of tension, anxiety, pain & basically anger at the world. I feel vengeful ... Sometimes I sit here & think about my family, my parents in particular, the after-effects are vividly real, my mother cries a lot ...

If Breda had come to some kind of acceptance, albeit with strong feelings of fear, loneliness and insecurity, the grip of grief on Frances had not loosened. She came home one year after Cathal's death and confessed that she

was a mess. I couldn't bear to be out of my mother's sight. I had a hard time leaving her at night. I was twenty-three years old. My life had disintegrated. I had to leave America. I had to leave the man I loved. I was terrified in the car. I didn't want to leave our home. I didn't want to talk to anyone except my family. I had no centre, no strength, no core. I was like jelly. I had zero confidence. I felt like a foetus. Completely helpless.

--- ----

CHAPTER EIGHT

Sad, Mad and Guilty

*A Great Rage at God, at the Driver of the Car
that Killed our Child, and at our Child himself*

U NTIL THE END of the first year the only reminder
of Cathal in the graveyard was the mound of clay.
Sometime during that year Mary and I had gone to see
the monumental sculptor, and made preparations for making
a headstone. My disbelief returned as I stood in the yard with
the sculptor, examining the samples that he had neatly stacked
along the wall, and then calmly writing out the inscription for
him. Seeing the inscription in black and white sharpened
those feeling of disbelief. Yet, despite the disbelief, this was
one of those events that reinforced the reality of our loss.

A few days before Cathal's first anniversary I went into the
graveyard to pray at the clay mound, and was riveted by the
sight of the new headstone. I stood rooted to the ground,
tears streaming down my face as I read the gold letters:

In
Loving memory of
Our dearest son and brother
Cathal O'Shea
Furze, Thurles
Tragically killed 18th Feb. 1990
Aged 13 years
Ar dheis Dé go raibh a anam

At last the loss was named for all to see. That simple epitaph concealed so much heartache.

The first anniversary came soon after. Choosing a photograph and writing out the words for inclusion in the local paper was painful in the extreme. Seeing his photograph in the obituaries of *The Tipperary Star* filled the whole family with sadness. I gazed at the innocent face and wept for our lost child. This would be an annual occurrence. But that first anniversary was crucial in my own healing. Not only was it an occasion to heighten my feelings of grief, but it also brought some relief. I had now experienced all the anniversaries. Surely, I thought, experiencing them the following year could hardly be as painful.

Like the rest of us, Breda had anticipated the first anniversary with dread, and felt a great sense of loss as she went through that day. The final entry in her journal on 30 March 1991 was, in a sense, symbolic. I found this entry very difficult. Heartbreaking. It symbolised the passing of all the anniversaries and special occasions; and perhaps the need to struggle on without the aid of journals or diaries. It is full of pathos, sad feelings and thoughts of what had been, and what might have been:

> It's more than a month now since Cathal's first anniversary. It was one of the worst periods of my life. Because I was not in a state of shock I relived the whole nightmare, totally aware of what had happened. The pain & frustration I felt were tremendous. Coming back to this city was very hard, & was something I would never have done had Mark not been here. I spent weeks in torment, wondering whether or not I should stay or go home, making life miserable for Mark, & crying every night. I didn't think I would last. I loved Mark but I thought if I went home I would still be in pain &

grieving, but I would be without the man I love. Since then I have settled down a bit, but I disagree with whoever said it would get easier. I feel so sad all the time.

When Cathal died a huge part of my life did too. He was my pride & joy. Oh God! I was so very proud of him. He was so witty. He used to say things to Dad that I wouldn't even dream of, & the little brat got away with it!

I remember all those nights he slept in my bed with me. He was on the inside because he was terrified of the dark, the night, the unknown. We used to talk for hours, him facing the wall & me with my arm around him, & my knees pulled up underneath his. We'd talk about my boyfriends & Cathal used to give me advice & the funny thing was, I listened. To everyone else he was an innocent child; to me he was my equal ... so uncannily wise ...

I could see us in years to come, inseparable. He probably would have come over here to me. Now those things will never happen. Every time I look at his picture & realise he's dead I feel like screaming. I still can't comprehend it, it's so scary. I'm desperately unhappy & it affects my whole life. That emptiness rarely gets filled. Mark wouldn't understand, & I couldn't expect him to. I love Mark very much. I like to just sit & look at him, follow all the angles and contours of his face, feel his hair, hold him close to me. I want to protect & look after him, but what he doesn't understand is that I was like this with Cathal. I used to gaze at him while he slept so peacefully, his little mouth open & his hair ruffled, damp with sweat.

When he was laid out in his coffin & I touched him, all I could think of was his damp hair & the tiny beads of sweat that clung to his little nose. All those memories are tearing away at me, & I can't explain them to Mark.

As the years went on we continued to experience many thoughts and emotions about our experience. Anger was one of the strongest feelings we had. It was intense in the early days, and continued to come and go throughout the years. It was directed at different times at the driver of the car that killed Cathal, at God, and at Cathal himself.

The feeling that I experienced of offering my child to Jesus as I looked at him dead on the hospital bed vanished. My spirituality and the importance of my faith to me became stronger, but I had occasional outbursts of anger at God. I suppose my faith allowed me to express my anger at God, secure in the knowledge that he understood.

Within one year and five months of Cathal's death, I was sufficiently healed to show an interest in the job of principalship of Our Lady's Secondary School, Templemore. I was, however, still in considerable pain, but I suppressed it to prepare for the long interview for the job. I read many books on educational management, having done two modules of a diploma in education in Trinity College, and did an excellent interview. When I came out from the interview I drove for about a mile and then the floodgate of emotions that I had suppressed burst. God took the brunt of the rage which I felt. I roared out as loud as I could in the car, banged on the steering wheel, and shouted 'F— YOU GOD'. I spent almost half an hour sobbing uncontrollably, and then felt the tension leave my body. I have no doubt that if the interviewers had witnessed that scene, they would have come to a different decision.

Mary, who was more ostensibly religious than me, did not find consolation in her faith for some time. It was not that she lost her faith, but that she was so exhausted and so anxious and uneasy that she was unable to find consolation in it. Unlike the rest of us she did not feel angry with God. She now gets much consolation from her religion. Bill, however, having wrongly blamed himself for Cathal's death, went on to rage at God for what happened to us:

> In a way God was also to blame for the death of my brother. After all, he is God and could have stopped this tragedy. I always believed in God ... what good was the church to me now? How could I ever pray to that merciless God again? Why could our so-called God not have done something? Why? Why? Why?
>
> My anger at God grew steadily. I began to lose faith in my religion; a religion which is vital at a time of loss. I watched how my parents let their faith help them, and wished that I could get the same help, but mine was not so strong. People kept saying Cathal's death was 'God's will'. What kind of merciless God would let Cathal die? He knew how we loved him. He knew what would happen to us if Cathal died. Yet he let him die. I could not worship this kind of God. I wondered if we were all fools for believing in such a God.

Frances also experienced this anger, and pointed an accusing finger at God, but with a more healing outcome that has seen her develop a deep love for God, always manifest in her life now:

> When Cathal died I blamed God. If he was the Omnipotent, why didn't he intervene? Why did he allow this horror? I cursed God. Literally, with the 'F' word – out loud too. I was not at all religious when Cathal died, so there was no comfort for me there, except to scapegoat God. In the days after, I desperately wanted to know where Cathal was. I just wanted to know that he was ok. I had a vivid dream that I believe was from God. It seemed absolutely real and I still remember it clearly.

In the dream I was on the couch in our sitting room looking at our family photo. Cathal spoke from the photo telling me he was ok. Everything was ok. It seems unremarkable, but it soaked my soul with comfort. I felt that Cathal had spoken to me. I believe God was telling me he was safe at last.

As that first year came to an end, and her anger at God began to evaporate, Frances began a journey that led to a deep belief in God, and an experience of his presence in her life that I find remarkable in its strength and steadfastness.

The anger we had towards the driver is clear from what has been written already. Mary felt this anger, but has arrived at a place of forgiveness now. Bill did not feel angry at the driver, and indicated that he sometimes tried to feel angry at her and 'thought it was unnatural not to feel anger at her'. My anger ebbed and flowed. I often walk past the crossroads where Cathal was killed. Sometimes I was filled with rage at the driver when I imagine his last second alive before the impact. I can picture him trying desperately to turn away from the car as it sped towards him. He had no hope. My spirituality seemed to compete with this anger. I felt that anger was a sin. After all, I had been taught that it was one of the seven deadly sins. Within a short time of Cathal's death I felt that I should meet the driver, and contacted Sr Maureen Fahey, a bereavement counsellor, to arrange it. I did my best to forgive her and embraced her in Maureen's presence. Mary did likewise.

My anger had greatly abated many years ago, but reliving that time, as I write this book, occasionally rekindles it. As the book progressed it interfered with my sleep. One night I was still awake at 2.00 a.m. thinking about the accident, and how it might have been avoided. Earlier that day Mary had revealed that she no longer felt anger at the driver; and this softened the anger that I was feeling at that early hour. I began to think about what it must be like to kill someone, and for the first time I began to feel some sympathy for the driver. Nevertheless, I still did not have much space in my heart for forgiveness. But, some months after the typescript of this book being sent to the publishers, my mind involuntarily returned to the driver. To my surprise, I found myself standing in her shoes, and imagining the horror she must have felt for a long time after that fateful Sunday in 1990. Nothing is so healing as the feeling of forgiveness. But Breda's anger at the driver is still strong, and she still feels a sense of panic when she sees her. To use her own words she still feels 'a lot of resentment'.

Although our anger focused on the person who killed Cathal, it is really about losing him. It has nothing to do with forgiveness or lack of forgiveness. I love God, and still can be angry with him. Anger and forgiveness may not be comfortable bedfellows, but they can co-exist.

We realise that Cathal cycled out from a side road onto the main road, and should have been more careful. This carelessness eventually focused my rage on Cathal. I have shouted at him, 'Why didn't you stop? You were old enough to know that you should have been more careful. Look at what you are putting us through. How could you have done this?' This rage was always accompanied by a feeling of love and helplessness. That anger is now gone.

Bill, too, felt a strong surge of anger at his brother:

> I was angry at Cathal. I cursed and screamed at him for being so stupid. Was he showing off on his bike? Did he not hear or see the oncoming car? 'How could you have been so bloody stupid?' Not only was I angry at him for dying, now I was angry at him for not coming back to us, if even for a few minutes.

Breda was imprisoned in a frozen grief, and it took her a long time to focus her anger on Cathal. It was also a part of how she came to understand what grieving was all about:

> A few years ago I went through a phase of being very angry with Cathal. It came out of nowhere. I feel now that it was a vital part of the healing process. I see that it is so important to allow myself to go through every emotion without feeling guilty. I would rage at him for leaving me. How could he do it to me? It took me about fourteen years to accept the whole situation of Cathal's death, to be able to discuss the day it happened. In fact I still will not allow myself to think about that day. It was suggested to me one time that maybe Cathal had been somewhat at fault too, and I was horrified at the thought.

Sometimes the anger we experienced was not directed at anybody. It was a raw feeling; a primitive rage that surfaced without warning. It was so strong that it could not be contained. I remember Bill being so enraged shortly after Cathal's death that he pounded his fists against the kitchen walls. I tried in vain to restrain him, and felt the powerful physical strength that was fuelled by this rage.

There was also a degree of guilt in some of us. Neither Mary nor Deirdre felt any guilt. Mary had been an excellent mother to Cathal and was satisfied that she had looked after him in every way possible. Deirdre revealed that she never had any cross words with him and never felt any guilt, irrational or not. I, however, felt very guilty at being so strict with Cathal, although my children would say that he got away with some things that they would not have. He didn't like school, but when I found that he was not working I watched him more closely and put pressure on him. I remember being exasperated at his difficulty with mathematics. One evening

I helped him with his maths homework and eventually slapped him in my anger at how he was unable to grasp whatever he was doing.

Bill had a deep sense of guilt. As he looked at reminders of his brother this guilt became painfully obvious:

His room? His clothes? His toys? His school books? Him? What about me now? I loved him but I never told him so. Oh, how I longed to tell him now; how I longed to hold him. Why was I not there to stop the tragedy? There is so much I could have done. It would have taken so little. I could have done some little thing if I was at home that day to distract him, resulting in a change of fate. But no! No! I had to be away. I always had to be on the move. I could never stay at home and devote more time to my family. But I should have been there. In a way I was to blame for the death of my brother.

For a long time, Breda suffered from guilt, an extremely irrational guilt. She felt guilty because she believed she had abandoned Cathal when she went to live in England at the end of September 1989, some months prior to his death. Frances, too, comments in some detail about the guilt that she experienced:

I wished I could have seen Cathal alive, even though he was in a vegetative state. I desperately wanted to say goodbye, and tell him what I had never said enough – I love you.

He was my baby brother and wild as a hare. I had big-sister syndrome and worried constantly that he would get into awful trouble as a teenager and adult. I thought it my big-sister duty to discipline him and save him from himself because my mother was so soft with him. I remember hitting him for cursing at her and shouting at him for making noise outside while I was studying. When he was alive I couldn't wait for the day I could tell him that I disciplined him to save him. I couldn't wait for him to grow up safely so I could tell him I loved him. I thought about that so often. I felt like a parent whose child's recalcitrance camouflaged the soft side of love to elicit discipline.

Of course, I know now that was not my role, but I didn't know it then. I was like a mother bear protecting her cubs with my brothers and sisters, because they had no other protection. My biggest grief is that he never got to know how much I loved him. Imagine I was waiting for him to grow up so I could lavish that love on him and joke about his wildness. But, he never did grow up. And he wasn't safe either. All my efforts to protect were futile. And I stole from myself what I could have had for consolation afterwards – a warm relationship with him. I felt so cheated by that, so helpless, and so guilty. Everything about it was unresolved and unfinished. And to some degree it still is.

CHAPTER NINE

Eighteen Years Later

*Coping or Healing? Integrating
Trauma and Moving on, but Never Forgetting*

S O, HOW ARE we now? Anniversaries and special occasions are still the strongest reminders of Cathal. The pain is much less now for me on these occasions. Nevertheless, Christmas is not the same anymore. I enjoy it, and love being with my children and grandchildren, but experience a vague sadness around it. I used to love putting up decorations, but only in the last few years have I got any real pleasure in erecting the Christmas tree. It reminds me of Cathal's excitement long ago, and so was a source of pain to me until recently.

It is probably true to say that I still think of Cathal once a day either when I say my morning prayers, when I pass the graveyard, or when I walk by the spot where he was killed. I am conscious of sadness at these times. But, it is not overwhelming sadness, and passes quickly. Nevertheless, I must admit that when I pass the graveyard in the darkness of a winter's evening, my heart is still sore. The loneliness of the winter darkness intensifies the loneliness of being without him. The graveyard seems a more lonely place in winter darkness.

There are also other triggers that bring him to mind, especially places where the focus had been on him at some stage in his life. As I was writing this book Mary and I took a few days off to visit Wicklow with Frances and her husband,

Bob. We visited Glendalough, and I felt so sad as I recalled how we had once brought Cathal there on a too brief holiday. I frequently thought of him as I drove through the Wicklow mountains and through some of the lovely Wicklow villages. My eyes filled with tears as I remembered his innocent childish delight at being with us, travelling in our little red mini-van, having his ice cream and his tea and cakes in small colourful cafes. Just before Christmas, during the time that I was proof-reading this book, I took some American in-laws for dinner to the 'Jumbo', one of the local Chinese restaurants. I sat at the table and suddenly recalled the evening that I had taken Cathal to this same restaurant to celebrate his thirteenth birthday in November 1989. I remember that he had earlier said he wouldn't go, and then, to my delight, changed his mind. I wanted the two of us to be together. I wanted him for myself. This was most unusual behaviour for me, and perhaps it was a distant premonition that I would never get this opportunity again.

I have a strong feeling that Cathal and I would have been very good friends, and I feel a great loss in that also. In losing my child and my would-be friend, part of me has died. I have grieved losing part of myself, of seeing some of my characteristics as a child buried with him. Losing a child has been compared to an amputation by bereavement therapists. But I am peaceful in so many ways. I have lost the driving ambition that I had to write books, to strive for perfection. Perhaps it is age, and perhaps it is the many hours of therapy I did when training as a counsellor. I am amazed that Cathal's death did not kill my ambition in those early years, and that I applied for the principalship of a large school so soon after his death. My only ambition now is to be as good a counsellor as I can; to sit and listen, and see the world through the eyes of those distressed people who come to me for relief.

Even after eighteen years my concentration has not fully

recovered. I believe that the loss of a child has long term effects in terms of concentration. It does have a humorous side too, as I am sometimes accused of being 'away with the faeries' by some of my set dance colleagues when I get lost during a set.

It was only natural that I sometimes experienced feelings of loss and sorrow when I was writing this account, and I felt wretched when I read the accounts of my family. I had not expected some of the physical symptoms to reappear, and was surprised when the skin peeled off my hands. But I have to emphasise that I have found further healing from re-experiencing the loss at a deep level.

I still find it painful to look at the photo album that I compiled of him, and I am unable to look at a video that Breda has of him. It makes the loss more immediate, although going through the album for this book has helped, and brought me closer to acceptance. Other people I know who have lost a child find comfort in talking about and dwelling upon every aspect of their child, including photographs and activities associated with the child.

All of us still experience sadness at important family occasions. Our children have got married down through the years, and we really miss Cathal at those celebrations. We are all conscious that he is physically absent, but we know that he is with us, rejoicing with us. A memorial candle stood lighting on the altar during the various wedding ceremonies, and Cathal was always mentioned in the prayers. I always seem to stare at the bright light on the candle, and when we hear his name during the ceremony it is painful for us.

Mary is still broken-hearted, but admits that she can be happy and enjoy herself. She loves walking, dancing and going on outings with the active retirement group. But Cathal is always in her heart. She visits his grave every Sunday, and carries his memorial card in her handbag. She talked to

Deirdre about the questions I put to them, and finds it too hard to deal with them, but she has talked to me about the less painful ones.

Deirdre admitted that she has healed to a good extent, although there is still a sense of yearning in her life. She does not altogether agree that healing is such an apt word. She feels that learning to cope is a better way of putting it:

> Now I think of Cathal quite often, not every day, but often. I wonder a lot what he would be like; would he be married and have children. Would he be working, and close by? I still miss him even after all of this time. I look at his pictures on the walls in the house, and feel the lads have really missed out on not having their uncle and experiencing his personality. I feel sorrow for families who are going through the early stages of grief. I can talk about Cathal without crying each time now. I often stand at his grave and wish I could dig up his coffin to see him again. This is a feeling I always have at the graveside. I associate him as being in the grave. I talk about him to the lads a lot. Even Brian [Deirdre's youngest child] knew who he was from an early age.

One barometer of how we are can be gauged from feelings arising when answering the detailed questionnaire that some of my children agreed to answer. Deirdre did not find doing the exercise of answering the twenty-three questions on the questionnaire as hard as she thought it might be, 'but I honestly feel it is worth spending this time remembering Cathal, and thinking about him. It is still upsetting reliving the experience, but no longer unbearable'. Bill has healed to some extent, but admits that he still has a long way to go, and it took years before he could speak about Cathal:

Sometimes we even laugh about some of the things he used to do, but the line between this laughter and the ever-threatening tears is indeed thin. If Cathal is in Heaven, and is capable of observing us, he must realise how much he was and is loved. We have learned to grow through our loss as a family. Since his death we have never been so close. Although we are a fragmented family separated by seas we live together in spirit. We have great love for one another and I know it is a life-long love. The loss of our brother and son has invited us to grow and love. The dissolution of our grief was gradual. We were not forgetting Cathal but the pain was receding.

Bill goes on to say that one of his main obstacles lies in the area of religion:

I still blame God to a certain extent. I still find it difficult to pray, although I do try to get something from attending church. I wish I could gain as much help from the faith as my parents have.

He echoes our thoughts in the conclusion of his account:

It is my belief that one never recovers fully from such a loss. One merely learns to live with the pain. Sure, I can laugh and have fun, but that dark cloud will never lift fully. It will be with me through my entire life. My brother will never be a grown man. In our eyes he will always be a thirteen-year-old boy – a thirteen-year-old boy who on the 18 February 1990 lost his precious life.

Frances seems to have healed well, but it was a traumatic and tumultuous journey for a long time. She explains what it was like:

I healed oh so slowly. I experienced gigantic waves of grief that harrowed out my heart. The only people who could inhabit these waves were my family. I was as bad after the first anniversary as when it first happened. The sorrow was just as acute, and maybe more.

Frances has found peace, and feels that

someday I'll know why. It's probably because we live in a fallen world, where bad things happen indiscriminately, and God does not manoeuvre us like puppets to prevent them.

Like Deirdre, she did not find answering the questionnaire 'as bad as I thought it would be':

I was dreading it and postponing it. The parts that made me cry most were thinking about how he would be now, and remembering how hard I was on him, how I never told him I loved him.

Breda has recorded in some detail how she feels today after burying her grief for at least fourteen of the eighteen years since Cathal was killed. All our family members worried about how the others were coping, and I feel relief that Breda has arrived at a place where she has integrated the loss of her brother to the extent that she has:

It is over eighteen years since my precious brother was killed. The ferocious pain of losing him changed me in so many ways. I often found myself wondering who I had become, and where the easy-going Breda had gone. I questioned my parental skills, whether I was loving enough, patient enough or even if I was capable of giving my children enough of my time. Being so consumed by my pain left me wondering would I ever be enough of anything anymore.

I no longer think about Cathal every waking moment. I am able to enjoy myself, to allow myself to laugh again, but it has been a very long road. I still feel so sad that Cathal will never know my children. My son reminds me of Cathal so much; the same cheekiness, his wit and wildness, and of course his fear of the dark ... Cathal would have loved my daughter. She is so full of love for her family and has a beautiful, contagious laugh. I sometimes imagine her wrapping her arms around him, like she does to my parents. He would be so proud of all his nieces and nephews. Time does not stand still.

Even today Breda finds anniversaries extremely painful, and her response shows her unique relationship with Cathal:

I cry less frequently now, mostly at the anniversary of his death and especially his birthday. I actually hate marking his anniversary, the day he died. I hate that such a black day should define him in any way. To me his birthday is the important date, three days after mine. When I was a penniless teenager he would drop huge hints about his birthday present and I would laugh so much. Most of the time I had very little money to buy him anything decent. Now that I have, the opportunity is gone. I really miss that. Buying flowers for his grave is something I will never accept, although I do it because that's what we do as a mark of respect, I suppose. He was a typical boy. He would have hated flowers. It will always be such a sad day for us. He arrived into this world prematurely and left just as prematurely.

Breda ponders on this unique relationship, and its impact on her grief. This is not to minimise the suffering of any other member of the family. It is merely the individuality of the grief response. We cannot compare one grief response with another. We accept how we are. This is how Breda puts her relationship with Cathal as one of the mediators of her grief:

> My siblings have always said how lucky I was to have been so close to Cathal, but losing him ruined my life for so long. At twenty-one all that closeness was wrenched away, and I was literally left with nothing. Most of my memories went the day he died, and to this day they have never returned. I used to drive myself crazy wracking my brain, trying to recall the conversations and laughs we had. But all those occasions died with Cathal. I cannot even remember his voice. I suffered years of guilt because of it. Here was I, his closest sibling, and it was all gone. Since then I have accepted it.

The hardest thing for Breda now is seeing the sadness in her mother's face whenever Cathal is mentioned. She feels that Mary's gentleness has made the loss all the more painful for her 'and for us as her children'. She is conscious of how Mary took such delight in Cathal, 'her youngest, her baby'.

When a child dies, not only is the impact on brothers and sisters devastating, but their pain is also increased by their awareness of each other's suffering. Breda puts this well:

> My siblings have suffered so much, too. You cannot put a name on that grief, or indeed a description. It is far too complex. I will always feel pain on their behalf, as they do on mine. Sometimes the pain in their eyes has been so great it would tear you in two. My brother Bill went to hell and back, losing his only brother. I will never

forget what he went through; what he bottled up inside his young self, how he probably still struggles with his emotions. I still find thinking about that almost impossible. And yet I know we have broken the back of it. We had to. We all have partners and families. What choice do we have?

Breda has achieved a certain level of acceptance, which is accompanied by a belief that Cathal is always near her, watching over her. In a sense, his death has given her a philosophy for living:

> Writing this has been very difficult. I may not have dug as deep as Dad would have liked, because I am still very afraid of digging up those overwhelming emotions, and because Cathal is so private to me. I will never forget being so out of control. The total helplessness. Every day was like falling into a nightmare; one you knew you couldn't wake up from. However, I cannot change what happened. I cannot bring back my gorgeous boy. Living my life is what is important now, and being a good wife and mother. I know Cathal is up there somewhere, always watching over us. I ask him every night to protect the children in our families, together with my parents. I have no fear of dying. I know Cathal will be there to meet me. Whenever I have to tackle something I am afraid of I ask him to help me and I feel very strongly that he does. We were too close for him to just forget, no matter where he is. That knowledge gives me great strength, and all that is left then is to live this life as he would like us to do, and to try and not have too many regrets.

We have healed as best we can. The sudden death of Cathal has engendered in us a sense of fear that we cannot prevent such a tragic loss. A dread that anything can happen to suddenly snatch away a loved one. It was this fear that turned into terror for me in the early days. For many years after his death I always felt apprehensive if the phone rang at an untimely hour. It was fear that more bad news was on the way. I would immediately think of my four remaining children or my grandchildren. That fear and those thoughts still lurk somewhere in the back of my mind even today, although it is much more muted. I don't imagine they will ever fully go away.

I have no doubt that my children have fears for their own children. Deirdre has noted this:

> I hated when Martin had his thirteenth birthday. I had strong feelings of loss once again. I felt Martin would be taken from us, too, at that age. I also felt it was hard on Mam when Martin reached that age. I dread the lads going out on their bikes on the road even now. I remember in the early stages after Cathal's death pushing Denis away. I was so afraid of getting too close to him in case he would also be taken away from me.

Breda, too, has this sense of vulnerability about the safety of her children:

> Grieving over Cathal sapped so much of my time and energy. I felt so drained for so many years. I was literally afraid of loving my own children, terrified that one of them would be taken from me too. I still worry about my children, especially when I am not around to protect them. What if one of them fell from a wall, cycled on the road without telling me, were taken from the front garden?

Because Breda's son, Cillian, has many of Cathal's adventurous traits, her fears for him are increased. As she says, 'I have to bury the fear that something awful might happen to him. He is a very adventurous boy, and I struggle constantly with that'.

Bill cannot even contemplate anything happening to his children. He said that he 'could not cope if this happened to either of them. I could not live through the pain'.

Frances does not have children but she too experienced a sense of fear for a long time:

> I'm aware now of the transience and fragility of life. Nothing is guaranteed. I lived for a very long time with a deep sense of dread. I think there's still some residual dread there. I also have a fatalistic streak. I believe the human spirit can endure anything. I'm sad sometimes to think that I could get through anything. I don't have children, so nothing can ever be as bad as this unless I lose a child. And I survived to be a better person.

There is also a sense of sadness when we see those men who were once in Cathal's class. I have a photograph of that class. A large group of boys wearing their school uniform. Now I sometimes see these men, all over thirty. We cannot imagine Cathal as an adult. They are mature men. He is still only thirteen.

What Helped us to Cope and Heal?

Family and Spousal Support in Allowing the Feelings of Grief;
Being Understood, Friendship, Spirituality, Hobbies,
Creative Grieving, Dancing and Diaries

A S WE SLOWLY struggled along our journey of grief
we tried to help each other, but we were hard put to
survive ourselves, and relied on others for help. We
all healed at different rates, and none of us are fully healed,
but can live happy lives. Time was an important, if not the
most important, healer. Healing comes slowly after the death
of somebody close to us. It comes particularly slowly after the
death of a child, especially in the early stages.

And then the years seemed to fly by. Each year I felt better.
That glaring light that had been blinding me when I awoke
every morning gradually retreated, became smaller and less
threatening, and finally vanished. It was one of the best
barometers on how I was healing. It was several years before
the sun started to shine again for me, and before I noticed the
buds on the trees in spring, or heard the birds singing their
joyful song of new birth. When the world of nature re-entered
my spirit I knew that much healing had taken place. Now
when I wake up in the morning, I do not think of Cathal at
all, except on particular anniversaries. I remember him for a
brief period during the day when I pray for my family or when
passing the grave. There is sometimes that vague feeling that all
is not right. It is not an intrusive feeling. It is just part of me now.

Talking to others was also very healing for me. It was especially comforting to talk to those who had lost a child. I knew that they really understood, even if their grieving experiences had been different from mine. I was greatly consoled by the many letters I received, and which I have stored in the attic. Many of these were from friends, some were from acquaintances, and some were from strangers who had lost a child. I re-read them when writing this book, and still find them consoling. It is a very good practice to write such letters to bereaved people, and I regret that I do not do it often enough. Such a small amount of time in composing such a letter brings great consolation.

The most consoling letter I received was anonymous and was written by a father, living in Dublin, whose thirteen-year-old son had died. He wrote it two days after Cathal's death. It has faded with age, and I would like to share it:

> I was very sorry to read in the newspaper about the dreadful accident that befell your Cathal, and as a father myself who has also had the sad experience of losing a thirteen-year-old son I know full well how you must feel at this time and write to offer you my most sincere sympathy and to pass on some simple thoughts that helped in my own bereavement.
>
> Each day in prayer I thank God for the continued unbroken link which we still have with our departed loved ones through Him. We take comfort from the fact that we can indeed talk to God, the One who is caring for them now and beneath whose gentle, tender love and care they are not lost at all but are now *safe*, truly *safe* – *safe* from all harm and suffering. Furthermore, because above all things *God is love* it most surely then must follow that someday we'll meet and be re-united with them again.

I think of the sunlight coming from its central source of power, searching and touching each and every person on earth every day *intimately* and *personally* with its warmth and light, and this helps us to understand more clearly how, in a similar way, God's presence can indeed be everywhere, with each and every one of us *individually* reaching out, sustaining and helping us in all our several ways wherever we happen to be.

My name as such would mean nothing to you – the *important thing* is to try and help you with these simple thoughts, thoughts that have helped me and which I can truly share with you as one who has also lost a greatly loved and loving thirteen-year-old boy.

May God bless, comfort, strengthen and sustain you and yours and may His peace be ever with you,

Yours very sincerely,

Geoffrey's Dad.

Being busy also helped. Standing in front of a class or running a large school demands concentration and attention and took my mind from my gloomy thoughts. I am a historian by training, and I love to write. Being immersed in interesting research is an excellent antidote to preoccupation with grief. I love reading history books, especially biographies, and allowing my imagination to experience the life and times of some famous person gave my mind healing space.

I took up set dancing about eight years ago, and found it changed my life. It added to my happiness, and I made many good friends. It is so healing to see club members who lost children often showing great humour. There are about forty members in our club, and six of us have lost children. We never talk about it, but I am frequently conscious of it, and sometimes wonder how they are. I suppose I feel a special unspoken bond with them.

Keeping a journal to record how I felt was beneficial, and on the advice of Sr Maureen Fahey, who gave me a few sessions of bereavement counselling, I wrote a letter to Cathal, which helped me crawl another few inches on the road to recovery. I regret that this has been lost, as I would have liked to share it with readers. It was a letter which expressed my love for him and apologised for any occasions when I had been hard on him.

Creativity can be helpful in dealing with grief. I like to write poetry, and I composed the following poem as I drove into the town of Thurles on Friday 20 December 1996, almost seven years after Cathal's death. I had celebrated the end of term with my staff in Our Lady's Secondary School, Templemore, and was in a happy mood. Then, without warning, as I arrived in Thurles, the bright Christmas lights reminded me of the darkness that had descended upon our household in February 1990, following a joyful Christmas when Cathal had given us the lovely fruit bowl. I felt my tears anew as I contemplated his generosity, and again felt bereft by the loss.

CATHAL

The Lights of Christmas make me sad,
For they remind me of my dead child
Who was a light in my life
And who passed from me
Like a candle
Quenched by the cruel fingers of fate.
Oh, how I hate to think of it.
That child reminded me
Of me
When I was young and carefree,
Wild, quiet,

Full of mischief and of glee,
Blushing with the bashfulness of innocence.
He was to me
Myself.
Six Christmases have come and gone
With each the easing of my pain,
But all the same, the memories remain,
And live within me,
And I see him every day.
I always fear that somehow
In the distance of time
Since he was placed in the cold earth,
Alone,
Waiting for me to come
And join him in eternal sleep,
That I will forget the sound of his voice.
And every day I listen carefully
To ensure that it remains with me.
For the voice is the sign of the spirit,
It is the essence of the inner soul.
And his voice was soft as silk,
Like the music of the rain in spring
It falls upon my hardened heart.
And no! I will not forget
As long as breath remains within me
That lovely sound,
Which echoed in our lives
For thirteen short summers
Before it died.

I suppose writing this book is a creative exercise, and while its prime purpose is to help others and validate their bereavement feelings, it has had a healing effect on me. When I counsel bereaved people I not only listen to their story but get them to recall as much detail as possible. The motto of no gain without pain may be a mistaken one in terms of physical well-being, but, handled with sensitivity, it is relevant to the mental and psychological pain of grieving. I felt great sadness when I read my family's ordeal, looked at Cathal's copies, books, stories, poems, cards that he had created for us, his caul, re-read the bundle of letters sent to us in 1990, the Mass cards, the report in the local paper, the funeral notice in the *Irish Independent* of 20 February 1990, and the file on the inquest report. Sometimes this whole process was almost overwhelming, but when I had come through it I felt better. It was in a sense a lesson in how to grieve and heal without the unbearable sensation of the real thing.

The most important healing agent for me was allowing myself to feel my feelings. Despite being busy I had to make some time for my anger, my depression, my anxiety, my loneliness, my helplessness, my terror, or my sadness. Even if I wanted to, and there were times when I did, I could not stifle them. They were too powerful.

I allowed my tears to flow. For many years we had a big solid fuel cooker heating our house. It had a large white top to keep in the heat, and Cathal and I had the bad habit of sitting on it together each evening after school to warm our backsides. After he died I used to sit on it, getting comfort from the heat; and hunched over crying uncontrollably for many months releasing the pent-up feelings that grew during the busy day. It must have been difficult for others in the house to have had to listen to the weeping of an adult male each evening for such a long time. But, most of the time, I cried alone. I felt my family had enough to deal with.

My spirituality was also a very important factor in helping me. I am not an outwardly religious person, but I have always prayed, sometimes absent-mindedly, but it has always been important to me. I personalised my prayers when the pain of grief was strong. I identified with Our Lady, who lost her son too. This consoled me. I felt we had something in common. I also prayed to my paternal grandfather, whose name I share. I have always felt that he watches over me, and he, too, suffered much bereavement, such as losing three children, one of them aged seventeen, as well as his wife who was in her forties. Sometimes I prayed desperately to them.

In a sense my prayers could never be answered. The sad road of bereavement had to be travelled. The sorrow had to be fully tasted. But, I felt Our Lady and my grandfather understood, and felt confident that with their help I would, some day, be happy. And so it was. I firmly believe that prayers will always be answered, even if it takes years for this to happen.

Her faith, too, was important in helping Frances to heal. Despite her anger at God in the early days, Frances, in some desperation, confronted him and is certain that he responded to her desperation. Her confrontation was quite explicit and forthright, and it began at the start of her journey home a year after Cathal died:

Right before I left America, I wrote a letter to God on the subway. I told him that if he really existed I needed him. I asked him to prove his existence, if he was real. I told him that if he did not help me I would die too. I asked a girl at work what she had that I didn't. She had a radiance, a peace and a joy that was alien to me. You could see it in her face. My question was ridiculous. Her answer even more ridiculous. She said 'Jesus'. I thought, 'Oh here goes another nut'. But I was desperate. I actually knew I needed superhuman help. She gave me a bible. When I went home I read every bit of it, and other books she mailed. Peter said to Christ, 'To whom shall we go, you have the word of truth'. I decided I would either go all the way with Jesus or not at all. I am not a person of half-measures. That began my healing.

Frances healed slowly through this spiritual avenue:

God healed me by degrees and only by going through the pain. No one accompanied me through that pain. No person. But Jesus did. My whole life changed.

She also found that her decision to come home for a year helped her to heal and to begin coming to terms with her loss:

Being at home for the year helped, too. I needed to be where he had been. I needed the love of my parents desperately. And they gave it to me, unconditionally. They allowed me to be broken and they never tried to fix me. I was glad about that.

Mary found talking to her children the most healing influence over the years. She told me that she talked and cried with them 'often until I was sick'. She also found enormous support from her siblings. Her family are very close, and support each other at all times. One of the local priests also helped her to heal.

Deirdre summarised what helped her best, and cherishes the unconditional and continuous level of support given to her by her husband, Denis, who has remained a constant in her life to this day. She says that the level of healing and recovery she has experienced comes from the commitment and support of close friends, her partner and, 'most importantly', family:

Time has helped to heal. Also the support of Denis in particular, who was always there when I panicked and cried, which occurred frequently in the earlier years. We talked so much about Cathal; we didn't bury the grief and feelings. Sometimes I would feel immense loss for a few days, and it did take time to share those feelings that were so severe with Denis. Then when I let it out, it did help. Myself, Breda and Frances talked about Cathal all of the time. We haven't stopped yet – he still feels a big part of our lives. Mam also opened up to us at all times. I don't remember Dad talking very much at all. The anger that I still feel towards the driver has hindered the healing process, although it has abated somewhat ...

Breda, too, found the love of her husband, Mark, the kindness of his family, and the closeness of our family the bedrock of survival, hope and healing:

My husband is the person who gave me back my sanity, my reason to live and my two beautiful children. He used to feel so helpless, knowing that no words could ease my pain. I was constantly frustrated that Mark did not know Cathal better, and yet all the times we spoke and I cried helped me so much in the end. What would I have done without him to console me? I have always believed that Cathal was my soulmate and that he brought Mark and me together. He knew that I would need somebody strong like Mark. Loving Mark opened up my emotions again, good and bad, and he suffered greatly through it. Today I can honestly say we have a beautiful relationship that can withstand anything, and for that I love him so much. Cathal did a great job!

I know in my heart that any other man would have walked away long ago. Mark comes from a very close and loving family. His mother is a very demonstrative woman and his father is such a lovely man. They have helped me in so many ways, even though at times it must have been hard for them. Any parent would want their son to be married to somebody without baggage, and I came with a mountain of it. But I have come through it to a great extent and I love them and I know they love me in return. Their easy-going manner around each other has been my solace for a long time. My family has gone through such pain together that I needed a release sometimes. And yet I love my siblings and parents so very much. We were always close, and closer now because one of us is gone. We will always need each other. After all, who knew Cathal better than us?

I had always worried greatly about how Breda was coping, but I was afraid to ask her. I don't know where this fear came from. Perhaps I didn't want to know the depth of her pain. But, some years ago, while we were walking among my native Slieveardagh Hills, I cautiously brought up the loss we had endured. I felt so relieved when she responded, but also alarm and anxiety when I witnessed her grief coming to the surface. She had buried it for so long that it erupted, and almost overwhelmed her:

> About three years ago I started walking on my day off with my father. Wonderful walks all over the county. We talked a lot about Cathal. It was very painful but it certainly helped me to bring my emotions to the fore. Physically it actually hurt. One day while we were talking about Cathal I started to hyperventilate and naturally panicked. I see that day as a huge turning point for me. I could finally see that my grief was so deep rooted that it was actually doing me damage. I knew that if I didn't fight back, and accept that he was gone, I would be allowing myself to struggle on year after year without

facing it head on. My one big regret is not seeing a bereavement counsellor. I think if I had I wouldn't have suffered as much guilt. I would have known that my feelings were normal, and I would have come to terms with the whole trauma much earlier on, or at least accepted that Cathal was not coming back.

Bill's brief summary of what helped him heal is extremely qualified, and dwells mostly on escaping the pain. I feel that he did not grieve well. I worry that this was partly due to the fact that I did not give him, a teenager struggling with the demands of an Honours Leaving Certificate programme, the time or space or emotional support that he so badly needed. Bill was also very close to Cathal, and explained that this was one of the reasons he was unable to write a portrait of his brother. He spent more time with Cathal than the others when Cathal began to attend secondary school. I recall often passing the two of them on their bikes as they cycled to school, and I have no doubt that Bill watched over him in school, although he admits that they had arguments, as all teenagers do:

> Have I healed? I have learned to live with the pain – I do not think I have healed. My life has been very busy since then. I worked in (company), I worked very hard in college from second year, I had a crazy social life. I joined (company), and made loads of friends. I worked very hard, and moved fast to where I now manage 200 people and a $550 million-per-year business. I got married, had two kids etc. etc. ... I do not think I have taken the time to heal.

This partly mirrors how I behaved in my grieving. I threw myself into intense busyness, writing books, preparing students for the Young Scientists awards, and coaching them for the Slógadh competitions. But somehow I found time to grieve. I can understand how Bill found it so difficult to face the pain of bereavement. He seems to have buried his feelings, and this type of defence mechanism breeds anger. Bill admits that the anger that festered within him in the early years had been very strong, and made him aggressive.

Our bond with Cathal is still as strong as when he was alive; perhaps even stronger because we are aware of how much we have lost. From an early stage I felt that he was watching over us. I am conscious of how our family has prospered and is happy and healthy. Deirdre, still in the throes of shock and grief, faced an interview for a job in local government soon after his death. She was successful, and still works for local government. All of our children have good jobs, and are happy and successful. Mary still manages the home, and I have retired from the principalship of Our Lady's, and now have a small counselling practice. I have no doubt that Cathal is happy at how we are, but I often wonder what he would have worked at, who he would have married, what his children would have been like, and what kind of personality he would have had as an adult, what kind of father, uncle, adult son, friend he would have been. All of these will never be answered. He will always be a thirteen-year-old child to us, although, as Christians, we believe that he has now advanced in wisdom and understanding beyond what any human could achieve.

--- ••◆••• ---

CHAPTER ELEVEN

Grief

A Normal Reaction in Abnormal Circumstances

T HE LOSS OF a child is devastating, irrespective of whether it happens through suicide, murder, drug overdose, accident, illness or any other cause. It is devastating irrespective of the age of the child, whether it is in the womb or an adult child. Of course these aspects are an extra dimension, and influence the grief. But ultimately parents and siblings focus on the child, now departed forever from their midst. Studies have shown that people who lost a spouse as well as a child testified that the loss of the child was much harder to bear. That is not to minimise the awful pain of losing a spouse or someone dearly beloved. But it is the testimony of those who experienced both, although I have no doubt that some people find spousal loss the more difficult to bear.

Grieving is a process. Sometimes it is a complex process, and generally it is a painful process. When the departed one has been loved, it is painful. The greater the love, the greater the sense of loss and pain. Sometimes the pain is so unbearable that we tend to shut it out. This is a defence mechanism, but it can only work for so long. We have to allow grief. In a way we need to facilitate it. That sounds so cold, but it is true. I am always worried when I hear people say that they have made a shrine of a dead child's room. It is, of course, very understandable, but it may indicate that the survivor is stuck in their grief. It is a prominent symbol that the person is not ready to let go. And how hard it is to let go! But restoring a room for normal use after a child dies is not always necessarily a sign that we have let go. It may be a sign that we have avoided the suffering of grief, a blotting out of the painful reality. Or it may be an effort to show that we are trying to accept the unacceptable. It may be a sign that we are trying to move on, even though we are unable to do so in the early stages. I should add that it is also a sign of unhealthy grief to give away all of the deceased child's possessions.

It is, perhaps, all about the bond between the parent and the dead child. There was a time when therapists tried to facilitate parents in breaking the bond. That was truly brutal therapy. The bond persists beyond the grave. Once a parent, always a parent. The letting go of a child is impossible. I have seen my mother-in-law, who was in her eighties, weep as she remembered the two infants she lost as a young woman.

I think that after going through the experience of grieving, and reaching some kind of acceptance, it is also good to normalise what happened. The death of a child is not normal, but it is important for others to see that the feelings endured are normal in the context of bereavement. The grief behaviour exhibited by our family is reflected in the literature on bereavement. I would recommend in particular Ann Finkbeiner's book, *After The Death Of A Child: Living With Loss Through The Years*. This work encapsulates a wide array of grieving behaviours from a cross-section of parents, whose children died from various causes.

At this stage I can cast a relatively calm eye on how we grieved, where we grieved well, and where we failed to grieve. Looking at all the accounts of my family, I see a family in chaos, and, despite keeping up as normal a front as possible and carrying on as best we could, this chaos continued for a long time. It healed slowly, so slowly that it was not perceptible to us as we went through it.

Overall, it is now clear to me that we suffered two major debilitating bereavement symptoms – Complicated Grief and Post-Traumatic Stress Disorder. Understanding these is important for those suffering severe bereavement.

Complicated Grief is also known as pathological grief, unresolved grief, chronic grief, delayed grief, or exaggerated grief. It has been explained as too little grieving immediately after a death, or too much grieving long afterward. The crucial factor distinguishing Complicated Grief from normal grief is the intensity and duration of the grief. Our family falls squarely into this. We grieved with the utmost intensity over a long period of time. The agony that we suffered is not tinged with self-pity; it is genuine and it is normalised under this term, Complicated Grief.

It is only recently recognised that severe bereavement can cause Post-Traumatic Stress Disorder (PTSD). PTSD has been defined as a normal reaction to an abnormal situation, and is an anxiety disorder closely related to panic disorder. Traditionally, PTSD was associated with catastrophic trauma resulting for example from military combat, terrorist instances, violent personal assaults such as rape, and so on. Our family's experience meets the two recognised criteria for PTSD: the person experiences a traumatic event that involves actual death to the physical integrity of self or others, and that his or her response involves intense fear, helplessness or horror.

Nowadays there is specialised treatment for this disorder, but in 1990 our plight would not have fallen under its definition. Perhaps if it had, we might have been greatly helped through our grief. Instead we had to struggle on as best we could, and some of us became stuck in our grief for a very long time.

The symptoms of PTSD are very recognisable in the accounts of our family. These symptoms are clearly defined, and the sufferer does not have to exhibit all of them to be diagnosed with this disorder. They include living in a nightmarish world, feeling detached, sleep abnormalities, feeling terrified, depression, loss of memory, hyper-arousal of the nervous system, severe anger, loss of concentration and anxiety. The evidence suggests that women are more susceptible to PTSD than men, and clearly in our case Mary experienced severe symptoms for a long time. I have no doubt that I suffered from it for a considerable period also. One pointer is that those with PTSD often throw themselves into 'normal' activity, such as work, as soon as possible after a tragedy, or can feel isolated and alone. These make sense of some of my behaviour after Cathal's death.

While complicated grief and PTSD were the two major diagnoses afflicting our family, making our grieving severe and long drawn out, the pattern of what we endured within those diagnoses falls within the normal plight of those struggling with loss. Bereavement psychologists tell us that grieving involves a wide range of thoughts, feelings, behaviours and physical sensations. Not every person grieves in the same way, but proper grieving must involve some of these thoughts, feelings, behaviours and physical sensations. These bereavement symptoms can be prevented by denial, taking strong anti-depressants, or the blocking of feelings. I have often heard people say how well so-and-so is doing after a bereavement, how calm and matter-of-fact he or she is. I remember talking to a man whose son had been killed some weeks previously, and he chatted about his work and what he was doing as if nothing had happened. In cases such as this the survivor is unable to face the pain of losing a child. It is too incomprehensible and too excruciating to face. But, the blocking of bereavement feelings and thoughts not only leads to complicated grief, but can cause intense anger, depression and somatic symptoms. Somewhere, sometime they must be vented, or illness will occur.

While feelings, thoughts, behaviours and physical sensations are part of the grieving process, I believe that allowing feelings and emotions is the crucial aspect of successful grieving. Because of the importance of this, I will briefly reiterate some of the feelings that we experienced. The initial one was shock. This cannot be blocked out, of course, and occurs in the event of sudden death. We were going about our normal daily activities on Sunday 18 February 1990, and suddenly this horror was visited upon us, and our whole world collapsed. All of us were shocked. Our systems were frozen, our feelings anaesthetised. This momentarily protects us and prevents us from being overwhelmed. Some of my family have described it as numbness.

Along with shock came the feeling of disbelief, which is also a thought. Of all the feelings that our family endured this was one of the most consistent, and all of us felt it. Not only did this feeling arise at the time that Cathal died, but it has existed all down through the years. To this day some of us will say, 'did this really happen?'; 'how could this happen?'; 'I can't believe that Cathal is dead'; 'this can't have happened'. Like shock, the feeling of disbelief usually accompanies sudden death. Sometimes it exists beside a realisation of the reality of what happened. In other words, 'I know that this has happened, but I can't believe it!'

Along with shock and disbelief, anger and rage soon made their powerful presence felt among us. Anger and rage are primitive feelings and cannot be subdued. The unfortunate person who manages to subdue them will suffer long-term depression and occasional outbursts of rage. Some of my clients call this a temper, and I always rearticulate it as rage to help them begin to explore it. Anger and rage must out.

Someone must be blamed. Older people, like me, were taught that anger is sinful, but anger is a normal, healthy feeling. It is a primitive feeling and does not stem from any logical place. Venting anger leads to good mental health. People often confuse anger with the unacceptable behaviour that may accompany it. We are responsible for our behaviour, and should find a safe way to vent our anger. The anger in our family lasted a long time; and all of us felt it.

Generally, bereaved people experience anger, except in the case of a liberating loss. A liberating loss is where the survivor feels relief at the death. This can occur if the deceased had been extremely ill and in great pain. It can also occur if the relationship with the deceased was poor, and especially if the deceased was abusive. Normally, however, the survivor finds it particularly hard to be angry with the deceased. But, this feeling will express its presence irrespective of the target. This book has shown that we were angry with Cathal for being so careless. Those who mourn a suicide victim often experience great anger at the deceased. These feelings are generally mixed with guilt, and the tormenting question, 'why?' always arises.

A lot of research has been done on guilt. Most bereaved people feel guilty. It is part of the process, and involves a sense of responsibility for the death. Parents of children who die suddenly feel more guilt than parents of children who were expected to die. Guilt was felt by some of our family members for a long time. Sometimes it is a good feeling, and relates to our conscience. In other words, if we wrong someone it is only right that we feel guilty. It was right that I felt guilty about smacking Cathal for his failure to grasp mathematical concepts. That is good guilt.

But in the context of bereavement it is often necessary to challenge our feeling of guilt. Bereaved people often torture themselves with unhealthy, irrational and self-destructive guilt based on faulty thinking. It can be seen as part of unfinished business, and may need therapy to bring closure. When closure has been achieved we must forgive ourselves, and leave it behind. We must learn to forgive ourselves and to love ourselves, and that means loving the shadow as well as the good side of ourselves. If we only love the good side, we don't really love ourselves.

Our family is a very tiny vantage point from which to study illogical guilt. But it is a valid one, nonetheless. Frances, Breda, Bill and I harboured such guilt, and clearly it does not stand up under scrutiny. Breda's guilt about going to England four or five months prior to Cathal's death is totally illogical. She knew that, but still experienced a strong feeling of guilt. What could Bill have done to prevent Cathal's death? How was he to know that Cathal would be so careless as to cycle onto the road? Was he to be eternally watching Cathal to ensure his safety? I felt guilty that I allowed Cathal a bicycle. That guilt is unfounded. A child has to be given appropriate freedom and the chance to develop. We cannot keep our children under lock and key. They must learn to live in the world, and that brings risks.

Should I have gone for a drive each Sunday so that Cathal would always be out of harm's way? Should I have forbidden him his bicycle, so that he would be safer? Guilt can rest on ridiculous foundations and yet appear logical, but it is an immensely powerful feeling, and it clouds our thinking. It is part of the many 'if onlys' that accompany bereavement that trap us in our guilt. It is a very difficult feeling to shake off, and it seems to have lingered with Frances over a long period of time. It is natural to feel remorse at the perceived lack of closeness to Cathal, but isn't it lovely to play the big sister! Wasn't it very caring of her to worry so much about Cathal. I was constantly worried about him, and aroused the ire of Mary and Breda by my worries. But shouldn't a father worry about his children! Shouldn't a big sister, with a great sense of responsibility, worry about her little brother! We must not be more or less than human in our behaviours. We are human, and we cannot be perfect.

Loneliness is one of the most poignant feelings that bereaved people feel. It is only natural to miss a person that we really loved; and the more we loved them the greater the loneliness we feel. We experienced great loneliness after Cathal died. We experienced it as we lay in bed, as we walked on our country road, as we stood by his grave, on happy family occasions, and even in the company of others. It was my constant companion for several years. This was sometimes accompanied by yearning, by longing for him to return and be with us once more. This can involve fantasising, and that is normal. Yearning can also be an indicator of the healing process itself, and when it ceases it is a good sign that mourning is coming to an end.

Yearning is also accompanied by sadness. I consider sadness to be a beautiful feeling. It is the very essence of our loving humanity. It is the spirit of our vulnerability. We were sad for some years, and it has existed to the present day whenever we think of Cathal. It is essential that we allow this feeling, because blocking it can lead to Complicated Grief.

I often think of the sense of foreboding I had on the day before Cathal was killed, and the experience that Breda had. I never really believed in such premonitions. I regarded them as superstition, but as I immersed myself in reading about bereavement I came to realise that these mysterious instincts are common among those who have experienced tragedies. The anxiety that began with this foreboding was magnified when the tragedy came to pass.

Anxiety is a common feeling associated with loss. It leads to unease, restlessness and hypersensitivity. I found this one of the most tormenting of the bereavement feelings. My senses were hyper-aroused; even the ringing of the phone rankled on my nerves. I was unable to rest or have peace of mind. It was accompanied by fatigue. I wanted to rest but was unable to do so. It was a kind of self-defeating cycle.

My anxiety was accompanied by a feeling of helplessness. Helplessness is often a feature of grief following the loss of a spouse. The survivor finds it difficult to comprehend how he or she will continue following such a loss. In our case it stemmed from our powerlessness to prevent the death of our child. This helplessness bred a feeling of pure terror, and terror is a strong feature of Post Traumatic Stress Disorder.

All these feelings plus the great sense of loss generally lead to depression. Depression, that gloomy state where the sun never shines, where motivation lies listless, where the desire to stay in bed late and disengage from the world is normal. Allowing the feelings associated with loss eventually banishes this debilitating state.

These symptoms and feelings are part and parcel of grieving, but the process is complicated by other factors. One of these is gender, and it was obvious that the males and females grieved differently in our family. The females clung together, talked and cried and consoled each other. There was a high degree of empathy between them. The two males trod a lonelier path. I did much of my crying on my own, although I was always willing to talk about how I was. I had this, probably misguided, feeling that my children had enough to do to cope with their own grief. I was also aware that they watched us closely, and I could see how worried they were about their mother. The pain of one family member, especially the mother, affects all the other members of the family. Grief ebbs and flows among the members, and allowances must be made for this.

Apart from gender, how we grieve is also determined by culture, and, while not as prominent now as previously, religious belief is an intrinsic part of Irish culture. It was certainly a strong part of Irish culture in 1990, and it was deeply embedded in people like Mary and me, born in the mid-1940s. Religion can have a positive or negative impact on how we grieve, but some evidence suggests that parents with a strong religious faith fare better in grieving terms than others. They suffer less anxiety and depression. Some feel that giving back the child to God is his will, and that he will be as good a parent as they were. It is inconceivable to most parents that their child is not in Heaven, and hence it fosters a belief in the existence of Heaven among them.

A strong anger at God may co-exist with strong religious faith. Sometimes this anger may last a long time. Apart from feeling anger at God, the bereaved may lose their faith on the basis that a loving God, and a God who was loved by them, allows such tragedies to happen. The negative thoughts following a tragedy may even cast doubt on the existence of God, and this loss of faith may continue for many years. On the other hand a strong religious belief may sustain the grief-stricken. The Christian faith is not only based on the love of God, but on the suffering of Christ, and the bereaved may feel that they are sharing in that suffering. I certainly felt like that at times, although I'm not sure that it ameliorated the pain I was feeling.

Religious feeling and spirituality can be related to the search for meaning in the life and death of a child. But, parents and siblings who do not have any religious belief also look for meaning in the existence and death of a child. Following Cathal's death, I became preoccupied in looking for meaning for his existence. When we live to adulthood, meaning is easier to see and define. But where is there meaning in the life and death of a child? What if an infant dies? What if there is prenatal death? Where is the meaning there?

Ann Finkbeiner found it difficult to find meaning in the death of her child, and none of the parents she interviewed for her book were able to make sense of the deaths of their children. She struggles with this concept. For her, death is the natural way of the world. Things have their time, but the death of a child is unnatural. It goes against the natural order of things.

I can understand that point of view, but I found meaning in Cathal's life, and I learned to use it when I had to deal with the death of a student later on. This student died in Our Lady's Secondary School. She was a beautiful child in fifth year; she collapsed in one of the classrooms at lunchtime and died shortly afterwards. I did not tell the students, to spare them the trauma and preferring them to be in the safety and comfort of their own homes before the news broke. This gave me time to think about what I would say the following morning, as we prepared a plan to support them. Sitting at my desk with my own bereavement casting its long shadow over me, I spent a long time pondering how I would explain to 600 young people the meaning of Linda's death. The following morning, as I stood in front of this big crowd of young people, some tearful, some unmoved, the following thoughts underpinned my words to them.

The meaning in the death of a child often lies in dying rather than living. As adults we find meaning in our religion, in our vocations, in our many relationships, in our philanthropy, and in our philosophy. But the impact of losing a child has an enormously greater impact on us than any of the above. Witness the huge numbers that attend the funeral of a dead child. It evokes some deep emotion in the human soul. It changed my life. I became intensely conscious of how people feel when suffering the pain of loss. Up to Cathal's death I would not have known. Now I am able to empathise with those who are suffering loss. I understand what it may mean. I have always loved my children, but following his death I became even more conscious of how precious they are. That is the meaning that I attach to Cathal's death. It is, I know, a very high price to pay for such qualities. I would prefer not to have paid it. But he died and I am a better person. I would prefer to be a worse person and have him back. But that is not to be.

Cathal's death has also prompted the writing of this book. Perhaps it will help some bereaved people. If it does, then his death will have added significance and meaning.

CHAPTER TWELVE

A Small Symbol of Acceptance

The Cotoneaster Tree: White Flowers of Innocence;
Red Berries of Sadness

I WAS GLAD as I neared the end of the writing of this book. Despite its healing effects, I am not a proponent of inflicting further pain on myself or on my family. I also believe in living, and investing in the future. Just as we must make an effort to grieve, we must also make an effort to live. Life goes on. We have only one life, and it must be lived. It is normal to feel hopeless in the midst of loss, it is normal to want to die at times, it is normal to feel suicidal; but ultimately it is normal to want to live as fully as possible. Perhaps it is a choice. We choose to live, or merely to exist. We choose to be eternally morose or we strive for the recovery of hopefulness and joy.

That does not mean that we return unscathed to normal life. The loss will be there. The wound will never heal. The future is affected, and for men there is a sense of loss in the broken lineage. Children take their father's name and the loss of a child means a break in the family tree. It is not a major factor, but it must be recognised. I suppose I was vaguely conscious of it as an only child, with few male relatives.

I am fortunate because, as a professional counsellor, I am obliged to attend a supervisor every week. Mary, my supervisor, supported me whenever I felt I needed to talk about it. She suggested that I plant a memorial tree as a sign of acceptance.

When she said this I felt a surge of sadness, as the emotional impact of such acceptance hit me. I realised that I still did not want to accept Cathal's death, even after such a long time.

But during the week following my session, I experienced a sense of calmness, and felt that it was emotionally right for me to plant the tree. I hoped that all my family would support me in that decision, and it was with some trepidation that I asked for their opinion. It was such a wonderful moment for me as they all expressed support for the idea. It was all the more wonderful because Mary brought home a bough and suggested that we look for that particular tree. Eventually she chose a different one, and made the choice of a drooping Cotoneaster tree. I feel so satisfied with that. I cut off a triangle in the lawn near the front gate, enclosed it with a slabbed path, and filled it with stones so that it is a lovely commemorative feature.

All our family gathered for this little celebration. Bill planted the tree and Frances composed a healing prayer, which she recited as he planted it:

Dear Jesus,

We gather together in your name to plant this tree in memory of our beloved Cathal. Lord, we remember Cathal's life today. We give you thanks for the gift of his life. We believe that some day we will all be together in Heaven. Jesus, even as you give life to this tree, give life to the places in our hearts and lives that died with Cathal. Wash over us with your life-giving Holy Spirit. Draw us closer to you and to each other.

We pray in Jesus' Name,

Amen.

I wrote a simple memorial poem for our lovely innocent child, which I read to bring our ceremony to a close.

White blossomed sapling
In the dark soil
Forever rooted in my soul,
Reminding me of my child
Our child,
Our brother.
Innocent, forgiving, and forever smiling
As the soft breeze
Among the hedgerows
Spreads its fragrance on the morning dews of Spring.
And you went away in Spring
To dwell forever where no wind of winter
Can chill your eternal spirit.
Your warmth is always with us
Breathing its love upon our wounded souls
Calming our troubled minds
With loving presence.

During this ceremony I watched the sadness in the faces of my children, and the tears running down Mary's face. I hope those tears and that sadness will help to heal us further. Our sadness is a reminder of what we have lost; of the fun, the innocence, the forgiving nature that left us in 1990. Yet, as we stood around the memorial tree I was conscious that somehow I had five children again. Five wonderful children. The Cotoneaster tree will be another reminder of our child. Its white flowers in summer will remind us of how happy and innocent our child was, and the red berries in winter will remind us of the sorrow we felt when he was called away. For Mary, the drooping boughs are a symbol of how the weight of our sorrow caused our spirits to sink eighteen years ago. When

Mary and I are asked by strangers how many children we have, we always reply four. But in our hearts we know we have five children.

Frances never omits him as a family member:

> I always count him among my brothers and sisters when I am asked about my family. I never add that he is dead, and I always speak of him in the present, because I believe he is in the present. Just not with us physically.
>
> I believe we will all be together again in Heaven. And I can't wait for that. I used to be terrified of death, but after Cathal died that left. I'm not afraid of dying, but of leaving those I love behind.

At the beginning of this book I gave portraits of how our family remembers Cathal. As I near the end I would like to share another one drawn by Frances:

> Cathal was a very quiet, gentle baby. He was beautiful. He looked like Mammy and Deirdre. I remember him smiling from his white baby seat. I remember washing him. Later he became a ball of energy, a whirlwind. He had a great imagination, and one little cap gun could transport him into cowboy and Indian land.
>
> He was constantly playing and making noise. He had a strong, unbreakable spirit. He never saw danger. He was mischievous and daring. He resisted being defined and confined. He did not conform to the rules of the O'Shea household. He was a law onto himself. He loved Mammy totally and he sat on her lap a lot, even when he got big.
>
> He depended on Mammy for love and ran to her for respite after wearing himself out playing. He belonged to himself only. He was independent and fierce.

Cathal was indeed a free spirit. A joy in our lives, as all our children are. For thirteen years he was part of our family in his human form. He is now part of our family in his spirit. He will always be part of us. He lives in our hearts, and we will never forget him.

I would like to close our story with the final words of Breda in the last entry of her diary. She mirrors our thoughts as we join her in reaching out to our thirteen-year-old child:

> Cathal is no longer here, my life is not as it was; it never will be. Sometimes I fantasise about being with him. Sometimes he spends nights with me. I wake up thinking about him, & knowing he's been here. Good night Cathal, my beautiful little brother. I love you my baby & wherever you are I hope you can feel it. Please pray that someday we can all be with you, & ask God to make our lives a little happier. I love you forever and ever. Your 'little red hen'.

Acknowledgements

I wish to thank my wife, Mary, and my children, Frances, Breda, Deirdre and Bill, for supporting me when I suggested the writing of a book on the death of a child. It took great courage for them to invite other bereaved people into the ravaged heart of this family, where they would see the chaos and the pain that reigned there for a long time. They are an honest, challenging, articulate and frank family, and it was most generous of them not only to be unopposed to the writing of this work, but to assist me in writing it. It is a family book. I wish to thank them from the bottom of my heart for allowing me to record their pain and their wide range of grief-stricken feelings and thoughts, so that other bereaved people may get a crumb of consolation knowing that we had suffered so much and survived. As I merged my own grief with theirs throughout the pages of this book, I experienced in a new and more comprehensive way, at a distance of eighteen years from the tragic event of February 1990, our devastation as individuals and as a family unit, our struggle to cope, and finally our emergence from the darkness, scarred forever, but closer and stronger in our now often unspoken grief.

I want to thank Mary in particular for allowing me to write this account. I know that in her heart she was not happy that so much pain was about to be resurrected. It was not possible for her to talk very much to me about how she had suffered. Her pain is still severe when we discuss Cathal. I am very grateful to her for allowing me to use her diary. There are times as I wrote when I have been distressed at the descriptions of how my family felt in 1990; none more than reading the pain of a kind and caring mother, who adores her children. It is only fitting that this love is returned with their unconditional love for her.

I cannot say how grateful I am to Breda for letting me quote from her diary. It is a wonderful, contemporaneous account of individual grieving. Like Mary, Breda finds it painful to talk about Cathal to this day. He was her pet. He used to crawl into her bed from an early age. She understood him better than all the others in the family. Reading her journal was one of the most painful aspects of writing this book. Breda hopes with us that this book will help parents and siblings, and only this hope prompted her to share her thoughts:

> When my father talks about Cathal, with reference to this book, I am reluctant to join in. My personal thoughts and emotions about Cathal are intensely private to me. They are mine, and I am only comfortable speaking about him to my family. His memory is so precious to me. I have never wanted to talk about him to anybody who didn't know him, who wouldn't understand or remember his beautiful smile, his gentle yet wild nature, and know just how easy he was to love. The only reason I am taking part now is in the hope that it will help somebody else. Otherwise, for me anyhow, this will be in vain.

Frances, Deirdre and Bill agreed without hesitation to help me with the book. I see this as a token of their love for me.

ACKNOWLEDGEMENTS

Bill worried about how I would feel as I recalled those early days. 'Do you really want to put yourself through this,' he asked me on several occasions. I would not have been able to put myself through it without their help. Frances, Deirdre and Bill answered, in as much detail as they could, a long questionnaire that I gave them. This was not an easy task as it brought them back to the events of 1990. I am also grateful to Bill who gave me an account he wrote some time ago about how he felt as he tried to cope with the loss of his only brother, who cycled with him to school every day.

I would also like to thank Mary, my supervisor, for her encouragement and her suggestion that we plant a memorial tree to Cathal. I want to thank all of my counselling friends for their feedback on the typescript. I am very grateful to Donal O'Callaghan and Marie Crean who journeyed with me through the long and difficult years of counselling training, and who offered encouragement as well as critical analysis of this book. Finally, I want to express my thanks to Mary Guinan Darmody, the archivist in Thurles Library, for allowing me access to the letter I wrote to the *Tipperary Star* a few weeks after Cathal died.

[141]